Sister Talk

Experiencing God's Love Through Christian Friendships

JENNIFER DUGGER

Sister Talk: Experiencing God's Love Through Christian Friendships

Published by Growing by Surprise
Printed in the United States of America.

All rights reserved. No part of this publication may be reproduced, stored in a retrieval system, or transmitted in any form or by any means—electronic, mechanical, photocopy, recording, or any other—without prior written permission of the author.

Unless otherwise noted, Scripture quotations are taken from the *Holy Bible*, New Living Translation, copyright © 1996, 2004, 2015 by Tyndale House Foundation. Used by permission of Tyndale House Publishers, Inc., Carol Stream, Illinois 60188. All rights reserved.

Scripture quotations marked NIV are taken from *The Holy Bible*, New International Version®, NIV® Copyright © 1973, 1978, 1984, 2011 by Biblica, Inc.® Used by permission. All rights reserved worldwide.

Scripture quotations marked ESV are taken from The ESV® Bible (The Holy Bible, English Standard Version®), copyright © 2001 by Crossway, a publishing ministry of Good News Publishers. Used by permission. All rights reserved.

Scripture quotations marked MSG are taken from The Message, copyright © 1993, 2002, 2018 by Eugene H. Peterson. Used by permission of NavPress. All rights reserved. Represented by Tyndale House Publishers, Inc.

Scripture quotations marked TPT are from The Passion Translation®. Copyright © 2017, 2018 by Passion & Fire Ministries, Inc. Used by permission. All rights reserved. ThePassionTranslation.com.

ISBN (paperback): 978-1-7374819-0-4
ISBN (ebook): 978-1-7374819-1-1

Cover design by PixBeeDesign
Flower artwork design by Natalie Pitts

To my three sisters, Janna, Stephanie, and Denise, who were the inspiration for this book. Thank you for always believing in me, encouraging me, and pointing me to Jesus.

Stephanie, Denise, Janna, and Jennifer

Contents

	The Beginning of a Conversation	7
1	What Are We Talking About?	11
2	You Have a Story Worth Telling	24
3	Life is Better Together	40
4	Stand in the Gap	52
5	Always Choose Grace	66
6	Words of Encouragement	83
7	Let Your Sisters Help	97
8	Show Me Jesus	113
9	Embrace Your Differences	126
10	You Are Called to Be a Sister!	142
	Acknowledgments	156
	About the Author	158
	Notes	159

The Beginning of a Conversation

Dear Sister,

One of the biggest surprises of my life has been the experience of writing this book. You see, I am not a writer by occupation or even for recreation. Before beginning this book, I had written only a handful of things that were not for a school project—some notes for a few speeches and an occasional journal entry. Overall, writing has never been my hobby or love. I am a math teacher at heart. I received my undergraduate degree in Mathematics and Education and then my Masters in Curriculum and Instruction. I have always had a passion for education.

However, God loves to use us in ways we never imagined. He delights in pulling us and stretching us beyond our abilities, all the while showing us how amazingly He equips us for whatever mission to which He calls us.

About ten years ago, God started whispering in my ear that He wanted me to write. I often put Him off, questioned Him, and flat out ignored Him. I would say, "I don't know how!" or "What would I write?" or "I don't have time." Occasionally I would pull out a journal and write some things down, but I never fully embraced this calling. Ultimately, I allowed myself to believe I must have misheard God. Surely, He did not really mean for *me* to write a book.

The title *Sister to Sister* echoed in my mind over the years. A few times, I chose to write a short blurb about my experiences with my sisters or how they had ministered to me. But I never put much effort into any of it. I was busy with life—kids, church, and other ministries. However, the COVID Pandemic of 2020 halted most activities. Everything slowed down, and, for the first time, I found myself bored, wondering what to do with myself. One afternoon, I laid down on my couch and prayed for God to help me see how I should spend my extra time. "God, show me what *You* want me to do."

Ladies, I have never before heard God's voice so clearly, "Get up and write a book about sisters!" Of course, this was not an audible voice or in a burning bush, like with Moses. However, it was unmistakable that the Holy Spirit was telling me what I should do. For the first time in all these years of hearing His gentle nudges, I knew I could not ignore God's prompting any longer. Though this task was somewhat scary and intimidating, I was immediately filled with enthusiasm and a desire to share everything God has taught me about the Sister in Christ relationship. So . . . I got out my laptop, found those snippets of things I had written over the years, and started writing.

I do not know what God has planned for this book. I *do* know that God has a purpose in mind and His plan is always good. Maybe this experience was just a way of God showing me how He can work in my life in ways I never imagined. Maybe it was simply a means to ignite a passion in me for

The Beginning of a Conversation

reaching out to the Christian women around me. Maybe this book will find its way into the hands of many, inspiring women all over to embrace their calling as a Sister in Christ.

Or friend, maybe this book was written just for *you*. Maybe God has something specific He wants to say to *you*, and I am merely a vessel He is using to pour into you today.

As you begin to read this book, I pray you will tune your ears to hear God's voice. Seek Him. Listen to Him. Pray for God to open your heart to whatever He wants to show you.

I see this book merely as the beginning of a conversation between two fellow Sisters. I hope it inspires so many more conversations in the future—between you and other women and between you and God. I believe much spiritual growth can be gained through purposeful conversation, sharing our faith, and the ministry of our words. In fact, that is why I chose the title *Sister Talk* instead of the previous idea of *Sister to Sister*. My sisters have spoken so much truth into my life, and I hope I am able to do a little bit of that for you through this book. So let's start talking...

Your Sister in Christ,

Jennifer

> *May the God of hope fill you with all joy and peace as you trust in Him, so that you may overflow with hope by the power of the Holy Spirit.*
>
> *Romans 15:13 (NIV)*

Chapter 1

What Are We Talking About?

*Of all the blessings sisterhood can bestow, I think
the greatest is to be known, really known.*
—Colleen Sell

Years ago, my sister Stephanie hosted a Christian women's retreat at her house. During one of the break times, everyone was chatting and relaxing together around her kitchen table. While they talked, Stephanie stood behind one of the ladies, gently playing with her hair, something she used to do with my sisters and me all the time when we were younger.

For Stephanie, the scene here was nothing out of the ordinary. She was simply being herself, treating another woman with genuine love and affection. Yet this small moment made a lasting impression. Days later, the woman commented to my sister that this was the first time she really felt like she belonged—fully accepted, embraced, and cherished.

Why did this simple action have such a significant impact? Stephanie had merely treated her like a sister, showing her sweet affection in a casual but intimate way that said, "You are precious to me."

We need someone in our lives who sees the beauty in us even when we cannot see it in ourselves.

This one act had touched a desperate place in her heart. Before that moment, she probably didn't even realize she had a hidden corner in her soul needing extra attention. After all, she was a faithful Christian attending a retreat with her church friends, surrounded by other women who were being kind and polite. However, Stephanie's one tender act of affection had ministered to her deep longing—a desire for a friend who gave complete acceptance with no expectations, guilt trips, resentment, envy, or expiration date—a longing for a sisterly relationship.

We all share that same longing—a need for genuine love, tenderness, acceptance, and affection. We all desire Christian friends we can depend on to encourage and support us through the ups and downs of life, love us unconditionally, and point us to Jesus. We need someone in our lives who sees the beauty in us even when we cannot see it in ourselves.

Ultimately, what we all need more than anything is Christ! We need to experience our Lord and fully embrace our identity in Him, but this is not an easy thing to do. We experience God as we study His Word and as the Holy Spirit works in us, but we sometimes require something more tangible to help us fully grasp all God wants to teach us. We are earthly beings who live by example and learn by experience. We need to see God's love in action, feel His patience, and hear His message with all our senses. Our Sister in Christ relationships are an avenue for us to do precisely this. Our Sisters can help us experience God!

"Sister in Christ" is a common phrase, often used so casually that maybe we never stop to think about its full implication. For me, Sister in Christ is a deeply personal term of endearment that means so much more than just a fellow Christian woman. I see it as a term of honor, a high calling, and a precious gift. The two parts of this term, both "Sister" and "in Christ," are significant; neither can be casually dismissed.

We need to see God's love in action, feel His patience, and hear His message with all our senses . . . Our Sisters can help us experience God!

"In Christ" sets the standard for this sisterly relationship. It is founded on the common bond of Christ, meant to glorify our Lord, and developed in His image. Without the "in Christ," you simply have a biological relationship, which may or may not be positive. Without the "in Christ," the bond is created by mortal strength and built on human standards—worldly and ordinary. "In Christ," the relationship focuses more on the One who unites the two individuals than on the human qualities distinguishing them from each other.

"In Christ" is the *how* and *why* of the relationship.

How do we develop this type of loving, selfless relationship? Through the power of the Holy Spirit. There is no other how. The Sister in Christ relationship does not try to persist by human effort but instead draws its strength from Christ.

Why do we cultivate this friendship? Because God calls us to love each other and reflect His glory in all we do. Christ is the foundation of who we are, and He should be the focal point of each relationship we build with a fellow believer. Our relationships with our Sisters in Christ are meant to be a light to the world, showing God's love to those who are not "in Christ." If we cannot demonstrate all the love and grace God has to offer in our Christian friendships, then how do we expect to do this with nonbelievers (1 John 4:20-21 NLT)?

If "In Christ" is the *how* and *why* of the relationship, then "Sister" helps define the *who*.

Who are we loving and befriending? It is not an acquaintance, a colleague, a peer, or merely a friend. The *who* is someone like family, closely united to us, a lasting relationship that is intimately familiar and goes beyond the casual. It is no accident that God calls us His children and uses the family analogy so often in the Bible. This family bond is central to the concept of our Christian relationships. Whether you realize it or not, you do have a

We Are a Christian Family

Jesus asked, "Who is my mother? Who are my brothers?" Then he pointed to his disciples and said, "Look, these are my mother and brothers. Anyone who does the will of my Father in heaven is *my brother and sister and mother*!"
Matthew 12:48-50

For all who are led by the Spirit of God are *children of God*.
Romans 8:14

I appeal to you, dear *brothers and sisters*, by the authority of our Lord Jesus Christ, to live in harmony with each other. Let there be no divisions in the church. Rather, be of one mind, united in thought and purpose.
1 Corinthians 1:10

For you are all *children of God* through faith in Christ Jesus.
Galatians 3:26

large Christian family, an abundance of Sisters in Christ.

The question is not *if* you have any Sisters. The question is *how* to develop a deep relationship with the ones God has purposefully placed in your life!

The *what* is one of the central themes of this whole book. What do we do and say? What do we think and believe? What do we give, and what do we receive in this relationship? In general, I believe this is the part we struggle with more than anything else. What exactly does this "sister" relationship look like?

At this point, you might be wondering if a really good friendship can be considered the same thing. In my opinion, mere friendship does not fully capture all God has called us and equipped us to be. We fellow Christian women were made for more. God designed us and purposed us to be not simply friends, but rather family...sisters...Sisters in Christ.

I believe a Sister in Christ is more than just a friend; it is one of the many ways God can speak to us and help us in our lives. So this book is about embracing everything the term Sister in Christ has to offer and translating that into the Christian friendships you have with women.

My passion for this sisterly relationship has developed because of a wonderful gift I have experienced—my three biological sisters. I am not an expert in relationships, and I am not a counselor. I have not done years of research on what it takes to be a good friend, nor would I consider myself a perfect example of a Sister in Christ. Instead, what I have to offer is my personal experience. You see, one of the beautiful blessings of my life is that my biological sisters are also my Sisters in Christ. They are my natural family *and* my spiritual family. This is a unique gift from God, which provides me with a perspective not everyone else has. I believe that is one of the reasons God has inspired me to write this book.

Many of you fully understand the beauty and blessing of a sister relationship. Others of you may have had an unpleasant experience with sisters or no experience at all.

For me, I consider my sisters to be my best friends. On numerous occasions, when other women have watched my sisters and me interact with each other, they have commented on how unusual our relationship is. They find it refreshing to see us getting along so well. Some have even asked us if we would adopt them as sisters.

I do not say this to brag or suggest my sisters and I have done something special to earn their praise; I fully see this as a gift from our Lord. In fact, when women say this to us, I am always surprised. (Because I promise you, we have had many ugly moments in our sister relationships over the years!) I have pondered what causes this reaction. It has left me with the conclusion that too many have either never had a sister or only experienced a sister relationship full of resentment, competition, and distrust. So, let me give you a small glimpse of what Sister in Christ means to me.

When I hear this term, the first thing that comes to mind is a vision of my three sisters. My mind is filled with images of the fun times and laughter we have shared through the years. I see Denise and me as children dancing in our bedroom to Beach Boys songs. I remember the joy of sitting on the kitchen counter intently watching as Stephanie pretended to be on a cooking show while she prepared a yummy dessert. I think about Janna coming home from college and always being such a comforting escape from the trials I was experiencing in junior high and high school.

I am the baby of us four girls, so I also fondly recall the numerous times my sisters took care of me over the years . . . and how often they kept me from getting into trouble with our parents!

As adults, I think about us sharing the latest funny moments in our lives as we sip coffee together or how we can turn the simple act of making a meal into an utterly hysterical event. At the same time, I am overwhelmed with the sacrificial love they have shown me and the wisdom they have imparted to me. I feel their compassion, cherish their perspective, and appreciate their service.

They are the people I turn to for support during my most trying moments and the women who encourage me in my relationship with Christ. My sisters love me even when I act unlovable, and they are the gals I call upon when I want to have fun. They are beauty and light to me and a precious blessing.

So, for me, Sister in Christ is not merely a common phrase I use but an experience I have had of God revealing Himself to me through these three women. Their guidance, mentorship, and love have inspired me to share those blessings with others. God has also brought many other wonderful Christian ladies into my life who have loved me as a Sister in Christ. Because of these women, I have a passion for helping others understand and cultivate this beautiful sisterly relationship.

In our world today, negative examples of friendship abound, and books line the shelves describing the hurt and pain female relationships can cause. Sometimes these books and examples are helpful, showing us where we've gone wrong and demonstrating the detrimental impact of our actions. Unfortunately, if we saturate ourselves too much with this negative, we can come to believe it is all there is. We can lose our vision and become jaded, accustomed to these less-than-ideal versions of friendships that were never God's intention.

Therefore, it is essential we also have a positive look at Christ-centered relationships, concrete examples of how our Sisters in Christ can help us flourish as a daughter of God.

In this book, I describe the many ways my biological sisters have ministered to me, providing a glimpse of what a natural sister relationship could look like. However, the point is not to stop there. After all, this is not a book about family relationships. The purpose is to see our Christian friendships the way God envisioned them—as family. To develop a deeper bond and a more meaningful connection. To embrace our calling as Sisters in Christ.

As women, we have diverse experiences with female friendships. Some of you have been blessed with incredible Sisters in Christ who have loved, nurtured, and encouraged you throughout your life. You have enjoyed primarily positive experiences with other women and generally feel uplifted in your friendships.

For you, the challenge may not be in overcoming negative feelings toward your Sisters but rather that you may have become too comfortable with them. It may be these relationships come so easily that you have almost started taking them for granted. If you are in this group, my goal is to inspire you to find new ways to deepen your relationships with your Sisters in Christ.

Our purpose is to see our Christian friendships the way God envisioned them—as family. To develop a deeper bond and a more meaningful connection. To embrace our calling as Sisters in Christ.

Honestly, just writing this book has challenged me to work harder in my own friendships. I have found myself being more purposeful in my relationships, dedicating more of my time and energy to "practicing what I preach," so to speak.

If you have been blessed with amazing Christ-like friends, then I hope you are on fire to share that blessing with others. Hopefully, the words on these pages will refresh your enthusiasm for loving your Sisters in Christ more fully, and you will eagerly embrace new ones you meet as well. Because, friend, there is a world full of women out there who need someone like you to love them and show them their value as a daughter of God.

Others of you come from completely different relationship backgrounds. You may have been deeply hurt by women or simply never have found any you could be close to. You may be new in your faith, shy and introverted, or struggle to relate to others. Maybe you desire to be a wonderful Sister in Christ but never had a good example of one. There could be many reasons why female friendships are complicated for you. If this describes you, I pray what you discover within these pages will provide a great starting point for you to begin developing beautiful Sister in Christ relationships.

Friend, let me be your sister today. I want to encourage you, inspire you, comfort you, and gently challenge you in your relationships with other Christian women. I invite you to peek into the window of my life with three sisters and discover how the Lord can use others to whisper His sweet words to you. At the same time, I hope to heighten your desire to love each woman you know and then equip you with specific ways to express that love with all the fullness God inspires.

You will be challenged to reassess your thoughts, open your eyes, adjust your attitude, strengthen your resolve, improve your words, and enhance your service.

As you read through the book, you will notice I often use the terms "friends," "Sisters," and "Sisters in Christ" interchangeably. I have done this purposefully to encourage you to think of your Christian friends as your sisters and remember they are your "Sisters in Christ," as well.

Consider this a conversation, one sister talking to another, sharing testimony, faith, and encouragement about the beautiful blessings of being a Sister in Christ. Use the questions at the end of each chapter to encourage you to think more deeply about your own relationships and as a springboard to inspire reflection and move you toward action.

So, grab your favorite beverage, cuddle up with a blanket, and maybe even invite a friend to join you. Then listen for God's voice and allow Him to show Himself to you as you engage in some "Sister Talk!"

> A free study guide and journal can be downloaded at **https://growingbysurprise.com/sister-talk**. It includes the reflection questions, scripture references, and a sister challenge for each chapter.

Reflection Questions

1. Make a list of the "sisters" in your life. Who are the Christian women you are around the most? Is there a woman God is calling you to embrace as a "sister?"

2. Reflect on both your biological and spiritual sister relationships. What do you cherish most about them? Is there any area that needs improvement?

3. Do you feel you get enough "Sister Talk"—opportunities to engage with other Christian women deeply and purposefully? What are the biggest obstacles to this?

4. Think about what you need most from your Sisters in Christ. Love, understanding, forgiveness, being known, service, wisdom? More specifically, in what ways do you need God to reveal Himself to you through your Sisters?

5. Do you have any wounds from other Christian women that still have not healed? If so, pray that God will specifically minister to you in this area and heal those broken places in your heart.

> *Behold how good and pleasant it is when brothers (and sisters) dwell in unity.*
>
> *Psalm 133:1 (ESV)*

Chapter 2

You Have a Story Worth Telling

Trusting our friends is a reflection of how much we are willing to trust the God who created them. Until we can trust God with our naked vulnerability it will be impossible to trust other people.
—Lisa-Jo Baker

When I was younger, I was extremely shy. In fact, my sisters love to tell stories about how my shyness would manifest around others. When I was two, we had a college-age young man living next door who would visit frequently. Even though he was polite and kind, I would quickly turn my face away when he came around, refusing to even acknowledge him. Supposedly, he was not the only one with which I acted this way.

As I grew older, I often wouldn't talk around anyone besides my family. Since my dad was a minister, I was expected to speak with adults at church regularly. There were times when my shyness came across a bit as rudeness and embarrassed my parents. Even at home, my sisters would sometimes find me hiding under a large desk, enjoying being away from everyone. When I became a teenager and young adult, I learned that hiding under a desk wasn't considered socially acceptable, but I still was the typical wallflower in social situations.

Once I reached adulthood, my shyness was still profound. I struggled to develop close relationships with others and found women often considered me a snob. Internally, I had a hard time believing I had much to contribute to any conversation, even ones with my sisters. When I was with others, I spent a lot of time worrying about what people thought of me and wondering what value I had to offer in a relationship.

I'm not really sure where those feelings originated. Maybe I internalized too many negative comments from my peers or was influenced by what television portrayed as valuable and interesting. It could be that my personality just was predisposed to those feelings. No matter where they came from, I am certain Satan did everything he could to accentuate and perpetuate those damaging thoughts.

Thankfully, over the years, God used my sisters to minister to my heart and teach me how much I have to offer—I am valuable. They spent hours listening to me and telling me how much they desired to hear what I had to say. Through the work of God's Spirit in me and because of my sister's consistent encouragement, I slowly found my voice, came farther out of my shell, and learned how to engage with other women.

And I am so grateful!

If there is one thing my sisters and I do often, it is talk. When my dad describes our gatherings, he says there are words all over the place. We talk when we are shopping together, working together, and lounging together. We talk nonstop every time we see each other. Amazingly enough, it is generally not small talk. We get right to the point—what is troubling us, the joyous experiences we have had, how our relationships with kids, husbands, and coworkers are going, and spiritual truths we have learned.

Our constant chatting is refreshing because we are real with each other. When we ask each other how we are doing, we are open and honest. That's frequently not the case with women. Though most of us don't intentionally deceive our fellow Sisters in Christ, we often find it easier to quickly put on a mask and allow people to see only a faint shadow of our real selves.

How many times has a lady at church asked how you're doing, and you've answered with "Fine," even though you felt overwhelmed, scared, or hurt and were struggling to even be at church?

We hold back for a variety of reasons. Maybe we don't want to burden someone or desire to hide our weakness. We may fear others will not think well of us if they know what is really going on inside our hearts.

On the opposite side, if we are thriving, we don't want

to appear prideful or come across as a braggart. We want to avoid making others feel bad if their lives are not going well. For whatever reason, we hold back. We opt for a short "Fine" or "Great" with a nod of our head and smile, instead of saying, "I'm wonderful! I've been sleeping really well, so I'm getting so much done around the house," or "Not so good. I feel like the walls are closing in on me, and everything is falling apart."

We convince ourselves it is best to not reveal too much and keep everything casual and light.

This is another tactic the Enemy uses to keep us from developing deeper relationships. However, I am thankful God is able to overcome the Enemy's schemes! He has used numerous people to show me how expressing my faith and opening up to people can be a powerful and uplifting experience. Most of the time, my honesty has been well-received and has even opened doors for building better friendships. Yes, you will occasionally encounter a person who brings you down, responds poorly, twists your words, or simply seems to be determined to misunderstand you. But we cannot allow those people to dictate our actions and hinder our relationships.

We all have experienced times when the words of others caused us to second guess ourselves. I remember a situation where a negative voice threatened to deter me from sharing my faith, and yet God brought about a beautiful end to the story.

One of the first talks I ever gave to a group of women

covered Christian leadership. Honestly, being much younger than many of the attendees, I felt unqualified to speak to others about the topic. Only months before, I had encountered an older woman at a Christian retreat who poked holes in my confidence. When I tried to share my faith with her, she looked at me and bluntly said I could not truly know about trials and hardship because I was too young. She continued to explain how what I had experienced could not possibly compare to her pain and suffering. Her words added to my own doubts.

Did my youth discount the worth of my testimony? Could I teach these women anything valuable about leadership?

However, God brought other people into my life during this time who encouraged me and helped me see I had a powerful testimony to proclaim. They reminded me how God can use any of us, even a young, shy woman like me, to speak His words to others. So I listened for God's wisdom and message and then spoke from my heart.

During the speech, I revealed my personal testimony regarding the emotional toll of infertility in my life. I discussed the ups and downs I experienced when I learned each month I was not pregnant . . . again, and the quiet devastation I felt every time one of my friends shared the news they were. I talked about the pain and humiliation I had felt after going through various fertility treatments, only to be told once again they didn't work. I explained how hard it was to understand why I could not carry a child, while so many women, who did not even care about having children, could get pregnant with ease. I detailed the internal war waging inside me and how God had been my strength and comfort through it all.

God can use any of us to speak His words to others.

Gratefully, I also was able to share the miraculous part of the story regarding how God brought me children through adoption. On the very day my husband and I began filling out adoption papers, we received a prayer request from our church about a child. This 21-month-old boy would go into foster care unless someone was willing to fulfill a voluntary placement for him while Child Protective Services (CPS) investigated. God made it clear to us that He had chosen my husband and me for this task, and we offered up our home. The little boy arrived within the week, and we immediately fell in love with him. We adopted sweet, red-headed Dalton about a year later.

Desperately wanting more children and finding it tough to put aside my dream of bearing a child, we continued with fertility treatments—in vain. Eventually, God pricked my heart and gave me the courage to relinquish my dream of having any more children, and I fully surrendered my plan to His will in this area of my life. I remember my mom asking me, "So what's your plan now? Will you try to adopt again?" I said, "No. I'm going to stop trying to do anything. I'm just going to see what

God has planned for me." I left the conversation with my mom fully aware that God's plan might never involve me having more children. But His perfect plan was already in action behind the scenes.

Only two days later, I received a call about a newborn boy, our Dalton's biological brother, who was still in the hospital and being removed from the mom's care by CPS. The caseworker asked if we would be willing to care for this baby during the investigation. Though wide-eyed with surprise, my husband and I once again were willing to take this uncharted road God was laying before us. Less than twenty-four hours later, we brought home four-day-old baby James, and he's been with us ever since.

Somehow, in my talk, I managed to connect my testimony to Christian leadership, but I really believe God simply wanted me to share my story—His story—with those women. When I finished the speech, so many ladies came and told me how they also struggled with infertility and other specific issues I had mentioned. What I said had helped them know they were not alone in their trials and had given them hope in their journey. And it wasn't because I delivered some perfectly written, amazingly original, eloquent speech. It was because I had been authentic and allowed God to use my story to proclaim His message of love, hope, and peace.

This story is only one of many. I cannot count the number of times someone has thanked me for finally revealing something personal in a Bible class or small group. Furthermore, I cannot think of a time when being real and authentic and sharing myself has ended badly.

Now let me pause here and say, ladies, I know many of you have been hurt deeply by other women's lack of compassion and understanding for the real you. Like the demeaning older woman who tried to invalidate my faith and testimony because of my youth, your fellow Sisters in Christ will sometimes say hurtful things and respond inappropriately to what you disclose. Unfortunately, because we are all sinners, misunderstanding, rudeness, and judgment are possibilities even in Christian circles. However, we cannot allow that to taint our interactions and relationships with our Christian friends.

I am not advocating baring all your deepest, darkest secrets to anyone you meet. Discretion is advised. There are times when it is appropriate to hold back or edit our response.

For example, if you are in the presence of someone who has proven themselves untrustworthy, you may choose a different situation to reveal something personal. Suppose the story you want to share involves discussing another person negatively (such as in marriage problems). In such a case, it is advisable to think about how it will affect everyone involved.

Be careful to speak respectfully of others and avoid simply gossiping. In fact, I strongly suggest praying for God's wisdom in deciding what to reveal to whom. However, we also have to be careful we don't limit the depth of our relationships because we fear being real with our Sisters.

I love the song "If We're Honest" by Francesca Battistelli. If you haven't heard it, I hope you will stop and listen to it. It is such a blessing. In the song, she reminds us it often feels harder and riskier to tell each other the truth and unveil our brokenness than it does to live in the dark and hide our mess. "If we're honest" with each other, we all build walls around our hearts sometimes. However, we must admit that uncovering our hurt and messiness gives our hearts the opportunity to start healing.[1]

> *We have to be careful we don't limit the depth of our relationships because we fear being real with our Sisters.*

We tend to fool ourselves into believing we are the only one who carries hurt and pain, even though we are surrounded by Sisters who are just as messy inside as we are. Yes, some women look like they have it all together. Don't let this deceive you; they have mastered the art of keeping their dirt well hidden.

On the other extreme, some wear their dirt where everyone can see. Many women know exactly how big their problems are, while others carry the terrible burden of thinking they do not have any problems at all. (If you are a woman who is so prideful you cannot see your own weaknesses or struggles, then that *is* a terrible burden to bear. I know because, at one point, I was such a woman!

I'll leave that story for another chapter.) Mess comes in all types of packages, but I am certain every one of us is full of broken pieces inside. We wouldn't need Jesus otherwise!

When we let down the walls and allow others to see our true selves, we also give others the opportunity to share God's truth with us, learn from us, and grow alongside us.

I feel so much better about my own life when a friend recounts a story about how she has gone through the exact same thing I have. One of my sisters recently told a story about an argument she had with her college-age son. She did not set out with the intent to give parenting advice or explicitly teach us or bless us in any way. My sister was merely sharing herself and helping us understand better where she was emotionally at the moment. Yet her story had a beautiful impact on me.

When we let down the walls and allow others to see our true selves, we give others the opportunity to share God's truth with us, learn from us, and grow alongside us.

You see, her kids are always so well-behaved around our family it is sometimes hard to believe they ever act not-so-nice with my sister. Her story helped me realize a truth in parenting—you cannot measure the success of your parenting by one incident; even terrific kids have bad moments occasionally. I found comfort in knowing that even she, someone I admire as an amazing mother, had challenging moments with her son. I was able to breathe a sigh of relief as I left her house. Her simple act of revealing something personal helped give me hope and peace in my parenting journey.

Though we have to be careful not to spend too much of our time venting about life's burdens and worries, sometimes simply sharing a little about the reality of your daily struggles can end up blessing others. About a year ago, I decided to do that with my small group at church, and it had a significant impact on our group.

My oldest son was fifteen and had just started attending a new school. Understanding how to parent a teenager can be trying at times, and my son's rough adjustment to his new environment not only affected our relationship but caused tension in my marriage, too. One night, after an especially trying week, I decided to talk about it with our small group.

Our members did not typically get personal; usually, we focused on the simple chit-chat of everyday life and the Bible study topic for the week. It was rare for anyone to completely bare their soul as I did that night. I revealed how much I was wrestling with the choices I made as a parent, how much I felt like a failure, and how greatly I needed everyone's prayers. I was apprehensive about how it would be received, so the response I got was somewhat unexpected.

Another couple started sharing about how they were having similar struggles with their teenage child. That couple, too, had been burying their hurt and was in desperate need of help, guidance, and prayers. During the evening, it was as if a wall was torn down, and everyone breathed a sigh of relief, realizing it was really okay to show each other our vulnerability. Our group was so compassionate and encouraging to both of us couples, and I left feeling a weight lifted.

However, the blessings from that one moment did not end there. As a direct result of our conversation, the other couple connected more personally with another family, who helped bring some relief to their situation. Weeks later, that couple told me how my willingness to open up in our small group had made a difference in the situation with their own teenager.

Our testimonies are powerful!

Think about the most influential and inspiring books, sermons, videos, and discussions you have experienced. I would be willing to bet that many of them involved someone's personal testimony.

The movie *Soul Surfer* tells the real story of a surfer who lost one arm in a shark attack, yet prevailed and learned to surf again in spite of her disability.

Sickness left Helen Keller in a world of silent darkness, but she didn't let being blind and deaf keep her from a life of happiness and accomplishment.

Corrie Ten Boom hid Jews during the Holocaust and suffered the horrors of concentration camps for it. She survived to tell others about the hope she found in God through it all.

The real, unfiltered testimony of a person's obstacles and successes is the most moving type of story. Learning how God provided for them, equipped them, protected them, or empowered them is so much more miraculous to me than any story someone could make up. When people share their stories with us, we feel connected to them, are inspired by them, and are often moved to action because of them.

Every person has a story worth telling. The real story is about what God is doing in your life.

Sister, you have a testimony to give, whether you realize it or not. Do not be fooled by Satan's attempts at making you believe *your* story is not very interesting, important, or inspiring. I promise you it is. It is not necessary to have an exceptional talent or have endured a tragic life event to minister to others. If there's one thing I have learned over the years, it's that every person has a story worth telling. The real story is about what God is doing in your life.

All of us have been called to be witnesses for Christ. We must share the good news with everyone. Romans 10:13-14 says, "Everyone who calls on the name of the Lord will be saved. But how can they call on Him to save them unless they believe in Him? And how can they believe in Him if they have never heard about Him? And how can they hear about Him unless someone tells them?"

The gospel message can never be told too many times, and it is not merely a message of a one-time event that happened years ago. The good news is happening every day in our lives. Part of sharing the good news with others is about expressing the particular way God is working through you and in you during the daily ups and downs of life.

How can you be a witness to what Christ has done for you without first being willing to tell how much messier your life would be without Him?

Reveal your hurts and disappointments, but also describe how your relationship with Christ is carrying you through them. Express your daily frustrations and how God has opened your eyes to a new perspective or given you an extra measure of perseverance. Celebrate your successes and miracles and how God has given you strength, power, and provision in those moments. Share the specific mission God has called you to and how He is equipping you purposefully and perfectly for that mission. Also, acknowledge when you're struggling to see God's hand in your life at all. Your Sisters can help.

Psalm 107:1-2 proclaims, "Give thanks to the Lord, for He is good! His faithful love endures forever. Has the Lord redeemed you? Then speak out! Tell others He has redeemed you from your enemies." Sisters, tell others how

God has saved you, redeemed you, forgiven you, and loved you.

Nothing good happens in the dark. God designed us for a life in the light. So, tear down the walls, step into the light, and let your Sisters behold the real you, because you are lovely and have a story worth telling!

Reflection Questions

1. Do you struggle to be authentic with your Sisters in Christ? If so, why do you believe you hold back? If not, can you pinpoint what has helped you with this and how you could help others?

2. What is the story or testimony you have to share? Can you put it into words, or is it just a feeling deep inside? Try to make it come to life. Name it. Define it. Write it down. If it is not apparent to you, think about how you have seen God move in your life, even in small ways.

Has the Lord redeemed you? Then speak out! Tell others He has redeemed you from your enemies.

Psalm 107:2

How beautiful are the feet of those who preach the good news.

Romans 10:15 (ESV)

Chapter 3

Life is Better Together

Friendship is an extraordinary and often costly gift from God, a beautiful reminder that we are not expected to do life alone.
—Sally Clarkson

One of the treasured times growing up with my sisters was bedtime. My sister Janna loves to tell the story about how she would come to get me out of my crib when I was a baby and rock me until I fell back asleep. She could not bear to hear me whimper in bed.

Later, I shared a room with my sister Denise, who was eighteen months older than I. We would usually find something to giggle about, and we would regularly hear our mom or dad call out, "Girls, go to sleep." I am not sure why, but things are always much funnier at night when you are supposed to be quiet and sleeping. There were very few nights before the last sister moved out of the house that I ever slept alone.

After our oldest sister had left for college, the rest of us would typically sleep in one bed together. Stephanie was about seventeen, Denise was twelve, and I was ten. We all had our own rooms, but somehow, we usually ended up in one bed before the night was over. Stephanie took the middle, and we younger two were on the outside—all cuddled up together. We often snuggled into a large Queen-size bed, though the size of the bed never mattered. Many times we squeezed into a twin bed. Now, this gets tricky when someone wants to turn over; we learned to all flip together in unison.

It would have made so much more sense for us to each sleep in our own bed; we definitely would have rested better. But we were not concerned with practical matters; bedtime was simply better together.

Bedtime was not the only time we chose togetherness over practicality. We cleaned the house, shopped, and cooked together. Everything was better together.

As adults, this tradition has continued. When we all travel to an out-of-town sports game, we do not take separate cars unless absolutely necessary. We pile into one car, even if we must go out of our way to pick someone up. If we are at a family gathering and one of us has to run to the store for an item, she seldom goes alone. Someone volunteers to go with her. A sister of mine has often ridden along with me for a long-distance trip—two hours to IKEA in Dallas or dropping a child off at camp.

We do not care about convenience; we simply enjoy spending time together.

In the last chapter, we discussed the importance of tearing down our personal walls and sharing our testimonies. To do that, we must spend ample quality time with each other. A long road trip is an excellent opportunity to get to know someone. It is remarkable how close you can become when you spend hours in a car together with nothing to do besides talk! Some of my dearest friendships developed in part because of long road trips.

Sisterhood is not about convenience, practicality, or efficiency; it is about relationships.

In one instance, a friend and I went to an out-of-town Christian conference with each other for a weekend. Another time, I traveled with a lady for a few hours to a camp counselor training session. In both of these situations, before the trip, these women and I were more like acquaintances. Having a chunk of time with no other distractions allowed us the chance to get to know each other on a much more personal level. Now, these women are two of my closest friends.

Sisterhood is not about convenience, practicality, or efficiency; it is about relationships. I am an extremely practical person, so fellowship does not come to me naturally. I must work on it daily. I tend to overthink things, which often leads me to overlook an opportunity for relationship time because it seems impractical.

I will convince myself not to call a sister to hang out because I think she is probably too busy, or I do not want to make her feel bad if she is unable to join me. I will tackle a task by myself, like reorganizing my bathroom, because I imagine she surely has things she would much rather do. However, that's not typically the case. We always have so much fun when we get together, no matter the reason.

One summer, my sisters spent hours helping me redecorate my bedroom. They know that decorating is not one of my best skills; making decisions about such things makes my brain hurt. So, they went shopping with me to pick out new bed linens and curtains and then helped me hang artwork on the walls. It was a lot of work, but we had so much fun doing it. I almost missed an opportunity for fellowship with my sisters because I had convinced myself redecorating would not be interesting for them.

How could I invite my sisters to come to my house to do what I considered work?

Fortunately, their perspective was that it provided an excellent excuse to get together. For them, the "work" involved was not a concern; they enjoyed sharing life with me and having a chance to talk. I have to continually remind myself that relationship-building moments are precious gifts God desires to give me. I must never prioritize practicality over relationship.

Our Lord designed us to have fellowship and meaningful friendships. Satan has other desires for our lives. He wants us to live in isolation. When we are alone, we can be swayed, manipulated, and deceived more easily, and we are much more vulnerable to his attacks. Also, he wants to convince us we are independent creatures who do not need anyone else. The more we force ourselves to do everything alone, the more we start believing we should not be dependent on anyone, including God.

Sharing life with a fellow Sister in Christ is not a distraction from God's calling; it is God's calling.

Satan desperately wants to keep us from those who will draw us closer to God. He will use whatever tactics he can to make us think we are not important, our needs are frivolous, or we are an inconvenience. So, we must actively battle against his attempts at keeping us from relationships.

Sister, you are not an inconvenience. You are not an imposition. You are not an interruption. Sharing life with a fellow Sister in Christ is not a distraction from God's calling; it *is* God's calling (or at least part of it).

In Leviticus 26:12, God declares, "I will walk among you and be your God, and you will be my people" (NIV). God wants us to live in close connection with Him. He wants to walk among us, and He desires for us to be His people. God wants to dwell with us and in us, and He shows by example that He values intimacy and closeness (John 1:14; 1 John 4:13). He asks us to abide in Him and then reflect the beauty of that heavenly relationship in all our earthly ones. This type of close connection only comes through daily, purposeful, meaningful experiences. So do not over-analyze whether wanting your friend's presence is impractical or unnecessary.

Building relationships takes spending time together, and building relationships is what God wants us to do.

The more we surround ourselves with women who are actively seeking a deep relationship with God, the better our own relationship with Him will be. Have you ever noticed how merely being in the presence of someone who is full of joy can suddenly spark joy in your own life? Listening to another woman express her enthusiasm for what she studied in the Bible can inspire you to dig deeper into God's word. Watching a mom interact gently and patiently with her disobedient child may help you learn better ways to minister to your own child's heart. Seeing a Sister approaching a mundane job with delight and passion might stir you to see your own tedious work from a new perspective. Noticing how a lady engages respectfully with her husband can provide a beautiful example for you in your own marriage.

There are so many ways to benefit from sharing life experiences with other women and watching how God moves in them and through them in their own daily environments. For our Christian friends to have this type of influence on us, we must be around them in common, ordinary ways, not only at Bible class or church events.

Simply being with another woman can sometimes ease whatever momentary frustration you are having at the time. The mere presence of one of my sisters can suddenly turn a completely trying situation with one of my kids into a truly laughing matter.

When my kids were much younger, there were days when all I did was deal with one chaotic moment after another. From kitchen spills and scraped knees to sibling rivalry and tantrums, some days, I wanted to go out on my porch and bawl because of the constant battles and difficulties.

Occasionally my sister would come over on one of those days. It's miraculous how all of a sudden, when the next disaster struck, instead of losing my cool altogether, I looked at her, shook my head, and laughed. She gave me a knowing smile that said, "Yes, my sweet sister, I know you live in a world of crazy right now, but it's all going to be okay." During these trying times, being with her made them more bearable, and I was able to see my personal chaos from a totally different perspective.

Janna sometimes will come to visit merely to distract herself from the current problem she is facing at work or home. She finds getting out of the house can help her refocus. She may stop by unexpectedly while I am in the middle of homeschooling or cleaning or cooking, but I am always excited to see her. Because, ultimately, being there for her and enjoying her company is more important than almost anything else I could be doing at the time.

Just as I am willing to make time for my sister, she is happy to do the same for me. I know you all feel the same way with your own friends. If your friend asks you to spend time with them, you will gladly go if you can. I believe most of us desire to be there for the other women in our lives in whatever way we can.

We must also remember it is okay to ask your Sister to be there for you, to give you her time and attention, without feeling guilty or worrying about the perfect timing. We have to be willing to honestly express where we are emotionally and what we need.

Sometimes I tell one of my sisters I would love to hang out but am too exhausted to fight the battle of gathering my kids and getting them in the car. So, she visits my house and does not mind the piles of laundry on the couch and dirty dishes in the sink. She may even get the experience of seeing a child streak naked through the living room because, with my sisters, they get the raw, unfiltered me.

Shouldn't that be how it is with all our friends? We don't have to be polished and put together. In all honesty, I actually smile a little inside when I walk into a friend's house, and it's messy, or I see a mom wrestling with a misbehaving child. I am not judging them or even delighting in their unfortunate circumstance, but it makes me think, "Good. I'm not the only one."

You should never convince yourself not to reach out to a Sister for time with them. Call your Sister just to drive with you somewhere. Ask a friend to come bake pies with you simply for fun. If you have a project you need to tackle and cannot seem to get started on it, invite a lady over to cheer you on in your endeavor. Or when your kids are driving you crazy, and you feel like you are losing your mind, call someone to come over and bring their own kids. I promise you, lots of crazy together is much better than doing crazy alone!

Don't be discouraged when an invitation is not accepted. If you put yourself out there or invite someone to do something, you may get a "No," or no response at all. When that happens, it is easy to believe you are unwanted, uninteresting, or unloved. I have had that experience plenty of times.

A few weeks ago, I was inspired to make some new friends in my homeschool co-op group. A field trip to a state park was coming up, and I thought the hour drive would be an excellent opportunity to get to know some ladies better. So, I made a Facebook post in our group to see if anyone wanted to ride with me to the state park. Few responded to the post, and nobody took me up on the offer.

I admit the lack of interest deflated me and almost made me reconsider going on the field trip at all. I decided to go anyway, and it ended up being a great experience. Everyone was friendly, and I met several new moms. God ministered to my heart and helped me see that their lack of response had little to do with me and more to do with their own needs, circumstances, or personalities. I must repeatedly remind myself not to take things personally and keep trying, asking, and inviting.

When I feel discouraged in making new friendships, I seek the Lord's guidance and comfort. I pray specifically for Him to open doors and provide opportunities for relationship-building. I ask Him to send like-minded women into my life who I can bond with, and I also ask Him to open my eyes to notice women *He* desires me to befriend. Most importantly, I pray for Him to help me persevere and maintain a positive attitude even when I do not see fruit in this area.

> *It is in the ordinary everyday happenings of life where we see God in action, working in the lives of our Sisters so powerfully.*

God is relentless in His pursuit of us, and we sometimes have to relentlessly pursue our Sisters (without becoming stalkers).

They need us. We need them.

It takes time and effort to build deep relationships, but the reward is worth it. It is in the ordinary everyday happenings of life where we see God in action, working in the lives of our Sisters so powerfully. Occasionally things get in the way, but we have to keep trying. The timing does not have to be perfect; neither does your house. Throw aside all practicality when it comes to your friendships because life is so much better together.

Reflection Questions

1. Reflect on the time you spend with your Sisters in Christ. Is it often enough? Is it quality time? Are there particular women with which you wish you spent more time?

2. What are the obstacles to living life together with these women? Are these obstacles something you can control (like your own feelings), or are they beyond your control (like work schedules)?

3. What actions could you take to spend more time with your Sisters in Christ?

> *A person standing alone can be attacked and defeated, but two can stand back-to-back and conquer. Three are even better, for a triple-braided cord is not easily broken.*
>
> *Ecclesiastes 4:12*

Chapter 4

Stand in the Gap

*Carrying burdens with and for others is
where we see the certainty of our hope.*
—Christine Hoover

Summers with my sisters were filled with memory-making adventures. With no schedules to keep or assignments to do, we were free to embrace our creativity and enjoy whatever activity our minds could think up.

During one particular summer, we spent much of our time at a neighbor's pool. This couple worked during the day, and we could go in through the back gate to swim. Stephanie enjoyed working on her diving skills. Still novice swimmers, Denise and I spent most of our time at the shallow end having underwater tea parties. Janna had a summer babysitting job. So fifteen-year-old Stephanie had the fun task of being our lifeguard. She kept us safe and introduced us to new games and tricks we could do in the water.

One day, Stephanie got the idea to use our floaties and try to walk on water. Secretly wishing we had that ability ourselves, Denise and I were anxious to see her succeed. Stephanie sat on the edge of the pool, put the floaties on her feet, and hoisted herself up quickly to attempt her amazing trick. Of course, it did not go as planned.

Instead of walking on water, she immediately flopped over and was stuck upside down underwater. The floaties slid from her feet to her calves, and Stephanie struggled to get herself back above water. Denise and I came to her rescue and helped hold her head above the surface of the water while we wriggled the floaties off her feet. Fortunately, we finally succeeded, and Stephanie was able to turn back upright.

During the moment, the situation caused panic and fear. Now, we laugh about it, and Denise and I enjoy recalling the time we little sisters had to save our big sis from drowning!

Our lives have been full of these moments when one of us has had to step in and help another because she could not help herself.

Do you ever find yourself weak or desperate, needing someone to pray for you, guide you, or support you just long enough for you to get your head above water?

During one such desperate time, I first heard the song "Standing in the Gap" by Babbie Mason[2]. While attending a *Women of Faith* conference, a chill went through my spine as I stood in a stadium full of Christian women singing the song's powerful message. The inspiring lyrics reminded me I have a sisterhood of friends all around, praying for me personally, lifting me up to my Father in Heaven, and "standing in the gap" for me during moments when I need extra strength.

At the time, I was having trouble in my marriage. I had frustrations with my husband I believed I could not really reveal or discuss with anyone. Out of respect for him, I did not want to disclose issues in his life that were affecting me, and I felt very alone. I needed prayers and desired wisdom, but I did not feel it was appropriate to divulge too much. I was living in quiet desperation.

So, when all the ladies sang those words, I felt they were singing to *me*, promising to be there through all my ups and downs and praying for me, even though they did not know the details of my circumstances. As I sang the song, I was also making a commitment to the other women to be there for them when they needed me. Over the years, the song's chorus has echoed in my mind many times, reminding me of God's calling to stand in the gap for others and allow others to do the same for me.

Though I have often heard the saying "stand in the gap," I did not have a complete understanding of its meaning until recently. I thought it was merely an expression Christian people created to help one visualize the idea of praying for someone or helping another in their weakness. I had no idea it had Biblical roots.

However, the phrase is used in Ezekiel 22:30. "I looked for someone who might rebuild the wall of righteousness that guards the land. I searched for someone to stand in the gap in the wall so I wouldn't have to destroy the land, but I found no one."

Upon further research, I learned that "standing in the gap" was used in ancient battle times. A wall was an essential means of protection for a city. If there were holes or gaps in the wall, the city was vulnerable to attack. To keep the city safe, someone would have to literally stand in the damaged space in the wall and fight off intruders.

So, when we stand in the gap, we are filling in a weak spot where the Enemy might attack our sweet Sister, and we are helping fight Satan off until our friend can repair her cracked wall.

When we stand in the gap, we are taking an active role in defense, being a source of strength and protection, literally putting ourselves between Satan and our Sister.

What a powerful image—seeing a friend standing guard for another in moments when she is too weak to fight for herself. When we stand in the gap, we are taking an active role in defense, being a source of strength and protection, literally putting ourselves between Satan and our Sister.

We are not pointing out what *she* needs to do to fix the hole in her wall. We are not telling her how terrible her hole is, comparing how big it is in contrast to another's, or lecturing her about why she shouldn't have holes in her wall! We are not judging, criticizing, scolding, or condemning from far away. We are in the trenches with her, helping and providing an opportunity for her to regain her own strength.

Have you ever had the experience of trying to dig a hole in the sand on a beach only to have the tide come in and fill it up with water? You dig and dig, furiously but fruitlessly, because you are constantly being thwarted by the rush of water. Or maybe you have done laundry with a toddler only to have them pull clothes out of a drawer or basket faster than you can put it in.

Some seasons of life are like this. We work faithfully and enthusiastically, but circumstances keep slamming us down, making it virtually impossible for us to fend off Satan's attacks. Sometimes we simply need a break so we can regain our footing.

Ephesians 6:13 says, "Put on every piece of God's armor, so you will be able to resist the Enemy in the time of evil. Then after the battle, you will be standing firm." Standing in the gap for your Sister in Christ is a way to give her a necessary break, so she has a chance to stand up, put on her armor, get a drink of water, and refocus her mind. Then she can get back to fighting the Enemy, stronger and able to stand firm.

So, in what areas is your Sister vulnerable to attack? Maybe she needs prayer but does not have the focus or discipline to pray for herself. Then you can pray for or with her during her time of weakness. Maybe she struggles to find the time to study God's Word or finds herself overwhelmed by where to start. You can text her daily scriptures to provide her this spiritual food. Volunteer to work through a Bible study with her, and gently guide her day by day until she is ready to study independently. Or it might be she is depressed or anxious, and Satan is attacking her value or resolve. Then you could give her extra doses of encouragement, positive reinforcement, and constant reminders of God's love for her.

Recently, when I needed some extra encouragement, Janna sent me a YouTube video of Charlotte Gambill talking about the walls of Jericho.

Joshua 6 recounts the time when God used an unusual method to help the Israelites defeat an enemy. God told Joshua to have his men march around the city of Jericho seven days in a row…just march and blow the trumpets, nothing else. On the seventh day, they walked around it seven times while the priest blew their trumpets. Finally, after a long trumpet blast and giving a loud shout, the walls collapsed, and the Israelites conquered Jericho.

In her talk, Charlotte reminded us we must sometimes circle a problem for a long time, all the while possibly seeing nothing change, before the walls finally fall.[3] Wow, I relate to that. Often, I have felt like I was working diligently but not seeing any results. My sisters have reminded me of God's constant work in my life, even when it is not visible to me.

When I first started homeschooling my children, it was quite an adjustment, and I was handed a large dose of humility. Even after years of teaching experience and a master's in education, I was at my wit's end. Nothing seemed to be working. I could not get my kids to do their work, and they didn't enjoy homeschooling the way I had hoped. Also, I was having difficulty controlling my anger toward them. I prayed daily for the ability to love my children and be a good parent, and I felt I was failing miserably.

At the time, Janna and I were studying the book of Esther. As I dived into God's Word, my eyes were opened to all the nastiness I had inside. It seemed as though nothing beautiful was being produced in me. I felt noticeably far away from being anything like Esther, not even close to the Godly woman I wanted to be. I believed I was being pruned, and I was looking absolutely wretched. One day I shared my feelings with my sister. She looked at me gently and said, "Oh no, Jenn. Just the opposite. I am seeing you blossom," and she expressed how she thought I was doing a great job as a parent, and she was seeing so much growth in me.

When we enter those seasons of marching circles around walls that refuse to fall, it is so easy to lose our resolve, lose sight of our vision, or even lose our footing. That is when we need our Sisters in Christ to stand in the gap for us.

When we get tired of doing laps, we often need someone to take the lap with us. My oldest son joined the cross-country team in ninth grade. He had his first meet only a few weeks after he began training. Needless to say, he was not in great shape for his first three-mile race. In fact, he started off the line limping from shin splints, but he was determined to make it to the finish.

The first few miles were challenging yet manageable, but then his body started to give out. His face told the story; the pain in his leg was unbearable, and he was ready to give up. Many runners had already finished the course, including a friend on an opposing team.

The young man saw my son's pain and discouragement and went to spur his friend on. Even with the exhaustion of completing the three-mile run, the thoughtful friend ran up next to my son and chose to run the last part of the race with him, encouraging him until he crossed the finish line.

What a perfect example of standing in the gap! This friend recognized my son needed more than some cheering from the sidelines, and he came alongside him and stayed with him until he had finished the race. That moment has been forever forged into my memory—when a fifteen-year-old boy embodied the example of true friendship.

We all have trials we need to be delivered from, whether it's a dirty house, messy attitude, or unhealthy relationship. Sometimes this deliverance takes years or a lifetime, and it means circling the problem repeatedly in faith. God didn't design us to circle our own cities of Jericho alone. We need our Sisters to take laps with us and maybe even walk for us when we tire. We need to remind each other why we are on the journey in the first place and keep God's promises fresh in our minds when we are discouraged.

While standing in the gap is often about meeting someone's emotional or spiritual needs, it may occasionally be much more physical, practical, and tangible in nature.

God didn't design us to circle our own cities of Jericho alone. We need our Sisters to take laps with us and maybe even walk for us when we tire.

When my children were little, going anywhere was a feat. Any mother knows that trying to get toddlers dressed and in a car for an outing is not easy, but the developmental delays of my two youngest made this especially challenging for me. They were both over two years old before they started walking independently, so I had to carry them a lot, and they were heavy!

During this period, I moved into the same town where my parents and sisters lived. We would get together frequently, and a row of cars usually lined the street. Without ever a request on my part, the unspoken rule was to leave the closest parking space for me. They, too, had small kids and many times were carrying in lots of items, but they recognized the extra challenge I had and took this small measure to help me out. It was not necessary or expected, yet this one simple gesture made a huge statement to me. It said, "We see you. We see the hardships you are facing daily. We might not be able to do much, but we can do this for you. We see you!"

In addition to the close parking space, they did not expect me to bring food to our family gatherings. I used to suspect they were not fond of my cooking, but later I realized it was simply another way for them to ease my burden.

Even the great heroes of the Bible required physical help sometimes. In Exodus 17:8-13, the Israelites were fighting against the Amalekites. Moses was charged with standing on a hill and holding up a staff during the battle. As long as he held up the staff, the Israelites were victorious, but the Amalekites gained the advantage as soon as he dropped his hands. Moses became so tired he could not hold his hands up any longer. So, Aaron and Hur found him a seat and stood on each side of him, holding up Moses' arms. What a humbling and inspiring image—to visualize this great man, one of the heroes of our faith, being so weak and needing friends to stand in the gap for him.

We may not be standing against an army, but we are fighting battles in our homes, marriages, workplaces, churches, and country. Maybe the garden is full of weeds that need pulling, or a serious health concern requires a complete revamp of our diet. Maybe life is too dry to find the words to pray, or we simply need someone to sit and help us laugh over lunch.

When we are in moments of distress, we may struggle to perceive God's faithfulness, truly feel His forgiveness, or believe in His goodness. We can help each other understand and experience these aspects of our faith that occasionally feel just beyond our reach. Sometimes we must be the one who makes these intangible things more perceptible to our friend.

Music helps me internalize concepts and ministers to my soul. There are so many great songs about friendship; they have a way of encapsulating all these ideas into words that stick in my head and heart. A specific song probably comes to mind when you think about friends. Along with "Standing in the Gap," some of my favorites are "Lean on Me" by Bill Withers[4] and "Count on Me" by Bruno Mars[5].

No matter which one is in your head now, you probably will notice all friendship songs typically echo the same message—friendship is about carrying each other's burdens and supporting our Sisters through hard times. My Sister in Christ should be able to depend on me to guide her in dark moments, provide a shoulder to cry on during her trials, and give her strength to help her carry on.

You will also hear another common thread in these songs—these moments of weakness are not permanent aspects of our lives, nor should they be. The goal is always to move our Sisters out of the dark places and into the light, from weakness to strength, offering just the right amount of guidance to help our friend stand firm and walk on her own.

Standing in the gap should not hinder our friend's spiritual and emotional growth but rather provide the perfect environment for her to mature and blossom. Just like a greenhouse provides a safe haven for plants to grow and thrive before being transplanted in a harsher environment, the support we give our Sister in Christ during vulnerable times allows her a chance to develop deeper roots so she can withstand life's storms.

Friendship songs also remind us how universal this need for support is; not one of us can endure it all on her own. Thankfully, God has provided us with a plentiful source of Sisters to give us this necessary help.

The goal is always to move our Sisters out of the dark places and into the light, from weakness to strength, offering just the right amount of guidance to help our friend stand firm and walk on her own.

Standing in the gap is more than just serving your friend. It is about paying close attention to both her spiritual and physical needs. I challenge you to really open your eyes to your friend, notice the obstacles in her path, and find a way to help lighten her load. Like the simple act of giving someone a close parking space, it doesn't take much to show your Sister in Christ you see her and love her.

Be her strength when she has none left; give her perspective when she struggles to see; share your faith with her when hers is lacking. Pray with her, study the Bible with her, take her by the hand, help her walk on the journey, and make the daily promise to stand in the gap for your Sister!

Reflection Questions

1. Recall a time when a Sister in Christ has stood in the gap for you or when you have stood in the gap for her. What was the overall impact of the moment?

2. Reflect on your current situation...

   Are you vulnerable in some way, needing someone to fill a hole in your wall right now? If so, can you describe the exact type of help you need? Who might be able to support you right now, and how could you ask her for help?

   Or are you in a secure place, a position where you can support another woman? If so, can you think of a specific Sister in Christ who might need you to "walk a lap with her" or "hold her up" at this time? How could you support, encourage, guide, mentor, or help her this week?

> *Carry each other's burdens, and in this way you will fulfill the law of Christ.*
>
> *Galatians 6:2 (NIV)*

> *Dear children, let's not merely say that we love each other; let us show the truth by our actions.*
>
> *1 John 3:18*

Chapter 5

Always Choose Grace

*Wise women tuck godly wisdom into the
words they speak and even more into the
words they choose not to speak.*
—Lysa TerKeurst

Stephanie, Denise, and I love to tell the story about when the three of us skipped school together. This was totally out of character for us because we were all excellent students. But sometimes, we just weren't in the mood to deal with the drama that happened at school.

On that day, Stephanie felt a little sick, so she asked to stay home. When we heard Stephanie was not going to school, Denise and I decided we wanted to stay home too. Instead of objecting, our parents merely cautioned us to be safe and make up our schoolwork.

That one day is a memory I cherish. We had such fun watching movies and hanging out together. When we became hungry, we decided to make a pear cobbler. The three of us went into the kitchen and worked together to prepare our tasty dessert. When it was ready, we managed to consume the entire 9x13 dish of cobbler all by ourselves; we didn't even leave a taste for our parents.

Whenever I recall this memory, I am so thankful my parents trusted us enough to allow this freedom. They helped us see that it is okay to loosen our grip on our loved ones and not feel compelled to oversee and critique every moment of life. That one instance of trust on their part created a lifetime memory for us, and it inspired us to trust each other as we encountered more stressful moments in adulthood.

With my sisters, when problems arise, we are always there for each other, willing to do whatever we can. Of course, we are imperfect and never love each other as completely as we should. We hurt each other's feelings or occasionally say something rude or tactless. We have moments of jealousy, impatience, lack of compassion, or even anger. However, these feelings are fleeting and never grow roots in our lives. We know they are detrimental to relationships and do not represent the type of friendships God wants us to have. Instead, we do our best to believe in each other, trust each other, and respect each other unconditionally, no matter how much life throws at us.

Families will always face storms in life. Christian families are no different. You and your Sisters will surely experience tough times—financial troubles, sickness, extreme job stress, death of a loved one, and simply the craziness of life. The attitude you have as you journey together through these moments is part of what will help you weather these storms successfully.

All of us desire to be kind and loving. We want to be good Sisters. (Otherwise, you probably wouldn't even be reading this book.) However, it is easy to find ourselves doing those things we know are hurtful—judging, criticizing, and resenting—if we are not careful and purposeful in our friendships (Romans 7:21-23). We must push aside the fleshly tendencies that threaten to harm our relationships. Sisterhood requires a conscious daily choice of grace, trust, and compassion!

Our response to our Sisters in Christ during hard moments can either strengthen our bond or pull us apart. It can help us feel the love of Christ powerfully or instead make a challenging situation even harder.

I have often experienced this in my own life, times when a friend or sister's response has made a significant impact on my situation.

Our response to our Sisters in Christ during hard moments can either strengthen our bond or pull us apart.

When Casey and I first adopted our daughter, Elizabeth, we could barely make ends meet, and one of my sisters stepped in to help. Dalton was five years old, and James was eighteen months. One afternoon, Casey was contacted about a darling seven-month-old girl who shared our boys' birth mother. I was at home with the boys, unaware of everything happening behind the scenes. I just remember my husband calling me and saying, "Jennifer, get ready. I'll be home in three hours with a baby girl."

Once again, our family was taken by surprise by God's unique plan.

We had no idea where we would put this little one. We had no baby food, diapers, clothes, or a crib for her. Financially, we did not have the resources to add another member to our family. I had decided to stay home with our children and was trying to finish my graduate degree at the same time, so we were a one-income household. We were completely unprepared and yet felt confident we should welcome this tiny, malnourished baby into our home. We were excited and willing to continue on this journey with our Lord at the wheel.

Still, I must admit I wondered how we would make it work!

Almost immediately, Stephanie and her family made the three-hour trip to our home to help us out. They took us to the store and bought us a substantial amount of groceries to get us through the next few weeks. They were so sweet and comforting, buying us not only tons of necessities but also some fun snacks, sweets, and our favorite drinks. I remember feeling embarrassed that we could not afford the groceries. From the outside looking in, we lived in a big house, my husband owned his own business, and we should have been better off financially than we were. But we were immature and had made some terrible financial decisions.

However, my sister and her husband did not lecture us about being good stewards of our money or try to teach us a lesson in responsibility. They never asked us how we got ourselves into this money crunch or how we would get ourselves out of it. They did not use the opportunity to judge us or question us. They trusted us—that we were following God's call and were making the right decision for our family. They believed the best in us and served us unconditionally.

I can't help but think how much harder the situation would have been if we had endured criticism instead of encouragement and love during such a stressful yet wonderful time of our life. I am so thankful I can look back on the memory with only fondness and a heart filled with love from my family and God.

The examples of this type of unconditional love are endless in my family. Janna has gone for long periods where she has volunteered to host almost every event for our family. Since my sisters, parents, and I all live in one town, we often get together for holidays and birthdays. Of course, someone must host these events, and that can be a tremendous job. She knows my sisters and I struggle to get our houses ready for these gatherings. Since she works from home, she lovingly serves us by taking over the task of being hostess, and she never complains or resents us. She relishes the fact that she can bless us in this way.

Denise helps with whatever need comes about. When Stephanie was overloaded with work in a college Calculus course, Denise took hours of her day to tutor her. Whenever my mom has needed yard work done, Denise's whole family has often gone and spent all day mowing and raking for her. When Janna needed a room painted in her house, Denise, her husband, and I all pitched in to help.

I could list so many ways in which we all take moments to stop and serve each other. The point of these examples is not to describe specific ways we Sisters serve each other. Rather, the purpose is to highlight the attitude we have in our hearts regarding that service. Sisters in Christ should serve joyfully and endlessly with no expectations, no resentment, and no judgment.

With my sisters, I do not ever have to worry they will resent me if I call for help too much or fear they will hold a grudge against me if I cannot serve them enough. They will not judge me if they think I am making a poor choice. Each of us trusts the other implicitly—that we are women of faith who are doing our best, even when that best may not be much at all.

We do not concern ourselves with how often we have given each other money (and if it will be paid back) or how many times we have hosted an event. We don't count up the number of times we have sat for hours listening to the frustrations of another sister or how many times she has or has not called us in the last month. We serve when we can, and when we can't help, we graciously accept the service of others.

More importantly, each of us trusts God and His Word. We trust that He is in control, so we do not need to worry about telling each other what to do; He will convict our hearts if we are sinning, and He will guide our path. We don't have to be our sister's Holy Spirit—that job is already taken. Our job is to be a friend, a support, an encourager, and a servant.

Another way we can show unconditional love is by giving each other grace. Sisters in Christ should genuinely believe the best in each other and not become offended easily.

In contrast, a person with a naturally critical spirit can allow resentment and anger to grow and thrive in their relationships. Have you ever known someone who interprets everything you do with a negative perspective instead of a positive one? You feel like you must explain every time you can't make it to an event, justify why you didn't answer the person's text right away, or apologize profusely for a grumpy moment. This negativism is especially wearing on a friendship.

A true Sister in Christ always assumes the best-case scenario. If your friend doesn't call, you believe she must be extra busy, and you do not think she has stopped being your friend. If your Sister isn't doing much to serve you or just does not seem to be there for you right now, then you believe she must be in a season of life where she needs more help than she can give. You don't judge or criticize her, and you don't suspect your friend has fallen away from God. Instead, you think of a way to help her out.

A Sister in Christ chooses to freely give to others the same grace she wants for herself.

Years ago, one of my sisters told me a story about how her husband was in a grumpy mood and how she was worried it was her fault. She confronted her husband, and he sweetly but directly said, "Everything's not all about you." What he meant was that sometimes he was merely irritable, sad, or distant because of something going on in his own personal life. Just because he might be taking it out on her somehow or because she was experiencing the side effects didn't mean it was her fault.

A Sister in Christ chooses to freely give to others the same grace she wants for herself.

That story has stuck in my brain, and I often remind myself, "It's not all about me."

Friends, it's not all about you either. When other women are critical, manipulative, hurtful, and thoughtless, or when they ignore you, tease you, or forget about you, it often has little to do with you. More often than not, it is a reflection of your Sister's own issues and not yours. So, don't take it personally, and just love her through it.

I have a friend that I made as a new homeschool mom. We have been friends for over eight years now. Sometimes we go weeks without seeing each other, and we rarely do anything outside of activities with our local homeschool group. We often go months without texting or calling each other. I have forgotten her birthday, and she has forgotten mine. In fact, recently, I completely lost track of time and forgot that her child was having major surgery. It was weeks later when I remembered and asked her about it. She wasn't even bothered.

She trusts me, and I trust her, and we take each other exactly as we are, with our forgetful minds, busy lives, and personal weaknesses. We know we can count on each other to be there when we really need it, yet we give each other complete grace when we fall short.

This type of grace is not something that comes naturally. It is a choice you have to make every day. You must choose the perspective that your friends are doing their best at the moment and are not trying to personally hurt or dismiss you, even if their actions seem to suggest otherwise.

A few years ago, I had an unpleasant encounter with a co-teacher in a homeschool co-op class. From my perspective, she had scolded me unnecessarily in front of a whole group of students. I felt disrespected and embarrassed. Those feelings turned to anger later that evening, and I considered writing her a very pointed email about how her actions were inappropriate. Instead, I prayed and took some time to step back and think about the whole situation. I tried to see the scenario from her point of view. Maybe she felt equally upset by my actions in class. Maybe she had no idea how her words had impacted me. I asked myself, "Will confronting her bring us closer to each other and closer to God?" Though my fleshly self really wanted to tell her what I thought, I had to honestly recognize that the answer to these questions was an emphatic, "No!"

God reminded me that I must give her grace and try to believe the best in her. He also humbled me and showed me where I could have done things differently during the class, too. Ultimately, I decided to forget the whole thing and just continued to pray for God to change my attitude toward my co-teacher. It took some time, but I can honestly say that I have no negative feelings toward her now. We aren't close friends, but we are cordial and kind whenever our paths cross. As I think back on this situation, I wonder how differently this might have gone if I had sent that email to her.

Though there are times when Biblical, thoughtful confrontation is warranted, our very first action should be to pray and rethink our perspective. We must always choose grace and forgiveness!

I have to actively look for the positive and try to see and believe the best in my Sister. When faced with the choice of assuming my friend is purposefully hurting me or instead accidentally causing me pain, I should faithfully decide to give her the benefit of the doubt. I must have a limitless amount of forgiveness, understanding, and grace. Even with my three darling sisters, who I trust completely, Satan can easily sow seeds of doubt in my mind. He will tempt me with anger or resentment if I am not taking my thoughts captive in this way (2 Corinthians 10:5, NIV).

This is why trust and a deep relationship with the Lord are so critical.

My oldest son plays on his high school soccer team. Every time I go to his games, I remember being there years ago when my older sisters' kids played. When their kids were in soccer, we all were much younger and had more energy. We were known to turn a soccer game into a memorable event. Our whole family would drive together, take up a considerable section of the stands, and eat out afterward. There was rarely a game where my parents and sisters were not present.

Somewhere in my mind, I envisioned this would be the same when my son played, but that is not the case. Though my family does try to make it to as many games as possible, the enthusiasm is not the same, and they rarely attend an out-of-town game.

It would be easy for me to think my family does not love my son or me as much or be offended that they are not putting the same effort into attending the games as they used to. I could get mad and make an excellent case for why my family just does not care about me enough! I could let a wedge be driven between us, but that would not be believing the best in my family, and frankly, it would not even be based on reality.

I must consciously choose not to be offended and recognize that their lives are all different now, with other priorities, circumstances, and abilities. It is okay to be sad that life has changed and miss the way things used to be, but it is not okay for me to turn that sadness into a reason to judge my family's actions or motivations.

I am a checklist type of girl at heart, one who delights in dividing things up fairly. My sisters even used to call me "Skittles Girl" because sharing a bag of Skittles when I was a child always involved evenly dividing up every color—everyone got precisely the same amount of each. I am not ashamed of my type-A personality, and I believe it is perfectly designed by God. It is often a blessing as a homeschool mom. However, I must be careful this tendency toward fairness and perfection does not leak over into my relationships.

Tally marks and scorecards have no place in friendships, only smiley faces and thumbs up!

Anytime I start making tally marks and keeping score, I am playing a dangerous game. The truth is that my sisters have sacrificed for me and served me way more than I have them. They love me completely and would be there at those soccer games if they could. Even if that were not the case, what would be the ultimate point of keeping score? If we ever start worrying about who has served who more or who owes who, then we are walking down a path far from where the Lord wants us to be.

Our perspective needs to be that God has sacrificed everything for us and given us more grace than we deserve. In response, we need to offer that grace to our Sisters in Christ every time we get the chance with no limits, no conditions, and no record-keeping.

Tally marks and scorecards have no place in friendships, only smiley faces and thumbs up!

The 1 Corinthians 13 "love" chapter is frequently quoted and regularly used in discussing Christian love. Sometimes reading it from a different translation can help us see it with fresh eyes and inspire deeper understanding. From the Passion translation, let me highlight for you some words and phrases to always keep in mind in your friendships:

> Love is large and **incredibly patient**. Love is **gentle** and **consistently kind** to all. It **refuses to be jealous** when blessing comes to someone else ... Love is **not easily irritated or quick to take offense** ... Love is **a safe place of shelter, for it never stops believing the best for others.** (1 Corinthians 13: 4-5, 7 emphasis added)

It is not easy to live out this type of love with your Sisters in Christ. It requires you to have a proactive type of love rather than passive. You are not merely reacting to problems you notice in your relationship. In your daily walk with God, you are asking Him to reveal *His* desires for your friendship and open your eyes to actions you never thought to take. Instead of hoping you won't hurt or offend your Sister, you are purposefully seeking to forgive, understand, and serve your friend.

In essence, you are looking for gaps in your relationship wall—vulnerable and tender areas requiring extra attention—and then finding ways to carefully mend and strengthen those weak spots.

Also, you must see your friends through God's eyes instead of from a worldly viewpoint. A Godly perspective helps you separate people's value and goodness from their actions. Recognize that even a deeply spiritual, faithful Christian will act unloving sometimes. You must choose to see past the exterior behaviors of your Sister in Christ and look for the beauty that lies beneath the surface. Adopting this perspective is like strengthening your muscles; it takes time, effort, and a willingness to surrender yourself just a bit.

When you see your friends through God's eyes, you will also recognize that each one is at a different maturity level. In some friendships, you will be the Big Sister, and sometimes you will be the Little Sister. When you are the Big Sister, you may be more spiritual, thoughtful, forgiving, or loving than your Little Sis. Your Little Sisters may not be able to see your perspective or even recognize the sin in their own lives.

As a Little Sister, I know I am years behind my own sisters in my walk with God, which affects how my faith is expressed in my relationships. But my sisters are gracious and respectful enough to allow me to grow in God's time.

Age does not always determine our Little or Big Sister status. Our maturity in our faith is influenced by so many circumstances—how long we have been devoted to following Christ, our environments, our experiences, our personalities, and so forth. Just because we encounter a woman who is mature in age, it doesn't mean she is a mature Christian. So, we must be "incredibly patient" and allow all our Sisters in Christ a chance to grow up.

When you fill the role of a Little Sis, you must have the humility to recognize your Big Sister's wisdom and insight are greater than yours. Listen to her. Learn from her.

As a woman of God, you must know at your core that your identity has nothing to do with your status as a Big or Little Sister, the friends you have, the number of hours of mission work you do, or the number of likes you get on Facebook or Instagram.

You have to understand your value as a daughter of God, and your whole sense of self-worth should be deeply rooted in your relationship with God, not your friendships. I believe this is essential to the Sister in Christ relationship.

When we feel secure in our relationship with our Heavenly Father, our earthly relationships tend not to be so fragile. Instead, they are stable and can weather the storms that come. Without a strong identity in Christ, a friendship will easily be torn apart by insecurities and selfishness.

Dear Sisters, believe the best in each other. Make the daily choice to be trusting and gracious, and forbid Satan a foothold in your relationships. Do not take things too personally or be easily offended. Remember, often, any ugliness that comes your way is a mere reflection of your friend's battle with sin and not a reflection of her feelings toward you.

Always choose forgiveness over resentment, thankfulness over entitlement, and grace over judgment.

Allow your Sister a chance to grow and mature in her own way, nurturing her and guiding her along the road. Trust she is doing her best, and if she's not, that God will speak to her heart in His time. Avoid keeping score or cataloging your friend's actions. Always choose forgiveness over resentment, thankfulness over entitlement, and grace over judgment.

Above all, put Christ at the center of your friendships and enjoy the peace He brings when you focus only on Him—His grace, His patience, His forgiveness, His compassion, and His love.

Reflection Questions

1. When you think about your attitude toward other women, would you describe yourself as mostly full of grace and patience or primarily full of resentment and judgment? Why do you think that is?

2. Regarding how other women treat you, have you been shown much grace or much criticism? Again, think about why this might be.

3. Under what circumstances are you tempted to be more easily offended, judgmental, resentful, or critical? Are there certain people or environments that bring out the worst in you? Reflect on ways you can combat this.

> *Accept each other just as Christ has accepted you so that God will be given glory.*
>
> *Romans 15:7*

> *Make allowance for each other's faults, and forgive anyone who offends you. Remember, the Lord forgave you, so you must forgive others. Above all, clothe yourselves with love, which binds us together in perfect harmony.*
>
> *Colossians 3:13-14*

Chapter 6

Words of Encouragement

Every word we say either illuminates or obscures the character of God.
—Jen Wilkin

My family has a unique but wonderful tradition for birthdays. Our parties may not be elaborate, with extravagant food and the most exciting gifts, but there is one thing every birthday party in our family has in common—the perfect card. We might not blow out candles every time, but we never forget to buy a card. A great deal of thought and effort goes into choosing the card, and then we add our own personal words to it.

Traditionally, one of us will buy a thoughtful card, hide it in an out-of-the-way location at the host's house, and then everyone takes turns signing it. We don't simply write our name or "Happy Birthday." We share our hearts with the one we are celebrating. In the end, the card is full of funny memories, descriptions of the beauty their lives display, and heartfelt thanks for the blessing they bring us.

The birthday card tradition knows no age limit. Even when our children are young, we write special notes to them. It gives us the perfect opportunity to show them the good qualities we see in them as they grow and mature and to build up their faith from a young age. Before they can write, our children watch and learn from us. As they grow older, they begin to participate with their own homemade cards and messages. It is inspiring to see our children join in this tradition and become excited and motivated by it.

I have dozens of cards saved from over the years, and each one of them reminds me of a quality my family sees in me that many times I cannot see in myself. They serve as testimonies of the impact I have had on them, often without even realizing it. On my birthday, more than anything, I look forward to seeing what my family will write on my card—it always delights me.

You may find it surprising (since I have written this book) to learn that I often think everyone else is so much better at this card-writing tradition than I am. Even though I feel such love and admiration in my heart, it is sometimes difficult to convey those feelings in words. When my mind is stuck and I struggle to think of what to say, I find inspiration from reading back over the cards I have been given.

So I have included a few examples here from cards I

have received over the last several years. Maybe they will give you ideas for how you can encourage and minister to your Sisters in Christ.

Notes from My Girls

I want you to know how very proud of you I am. You have allowed the Lord to transform you—to take your weaknesses and use them for His glory. You have allowed Him to be your strength and your song . . . and you have done that with a smile on your face and a skip in your step. I am so thankful for you. You are a mighty warrior—a mighty woman of God! —*Steph*

What a blessing you are—a ray of sunshine to everyone who is in your presence. You let the Lord's strength and beauty flow through you—and it's magnificent to behold. I adore you, little sister. —*Denise*

You are a ministering angel in your little family and often to me also. Your strong, rooted righteousness is beautiful. Your love is strong, big, funny, straightforward, and dependable. I love you so much. —*Janna*

The Lord chose you to be the mother of those three children. He has equipped you fully to deal with what may be ahead in each of their journeys. We know at times you are tired and wonder if you are doing what is needed. Always remember they are not in Your hands . . . they are in the hands of the Master Parent. He will continue to guide you as you seek His wisdom. —*Mother*

Reading them, you might think I am the most amazing, faithful, perfect Christian woman in the world. I promise you, I am not. In fact, I would never write those words about myself. That is what is so powerful about words of encouragement. They show me what my family sees when they look at me, not what I see in myself. I may not feel like I have strength and beauty, but my family does, and the mere fact that they see these qualities in me has a transformational power in my life. The more they tell me I am "a mighty warrior," the more I become "a mighty warrior."

I have heard people tell stories of how they speak words over their children, telling them who they are in Christ and the influence this has on their children. They tell their child they are strong and courageous, so the child becomes strong and courageous. They tell their child they are beautiful, so they grow up feeling beautiful. It is incredible how impactful words can be. We often become what we believe we are.

We are highly influenced by positive words of encouragement and, in contrast, just as deflated by negative ones. We know what the Bible says about our identity and value. But let's face it, Satan does a great job of warping our thoughts, filling our heads with condemnation, and doing everything in his power to make us doubt God's complete delight in us. It makes a difference when someone who knows us well expresses something extraordinary about us personally.

We need to be known, with all our weaknesses *and*

strengths. It feels good when we tear down the walls and let people behold the real you. It's comforting to know people love us in spite of our flaws, but we don't need our faults and failures to be the focus of anyone's words. What we need is a whole lot of positivity!

We tend to have a heightened awareness of our own weaknesses or deficits, and it is easy to think everyone else readily sees those same qualities in us. It is hard to fathom that another person could see beauty where we only see flaws. I remember this happened when I had my Senior photos taken in high school. When I showed them to others, people thought they were lovely pictures. Yet when I looked at them, all I could see was my scrawny neck and ears that stuck out.

Now I can look back on those photos with more objectivity and recognize that they were wonderful pictures. Especially now that I am starting to gray and wrinkle a bit, I desperately wish I still looked that good! However, at the time, you could not convince me I looked beautiful in those photos. The negative voices of my insecurity overshadowed any kind words of others. And yet, those kind words did stick in my head and had a lasting effect, helping my future self feel more lovely as I grew up.

I have heard it said that it takes nine positive statements to counteract one negative one. Whether this is scientifically accurate or not, it certainly rings true in my own life. That is why we Sisters in Christ must be intentional about sharing uplifting, encouraging words with each other as often as possible. Really, we can't overdo it. There is no limit to how many times your Sister needs to be reminded of her value and beauty.

Sometimes these words of encouragement come in the form of stories we share or passing comments we might add into a regular conversation. They do not have to be well-thought-out lines or perfectly written letters. They do not have to represent every good thing you see in your Sister or encompass all your thoughts. Often the most impactful words are spontaneous, communicating what you notice in your friend at the moment. To do this, we must open our eyes and intentionally look for these beautiful qualities in our Sisters.

There is no limit to how many times your Sister needs to be reminded of her value and beauty.

When I think about a story my sister told about me recently, I chuckle because her perspective of the situation was so different from mine. The other day Janna recounted when my husband brought home eighteen baby chicks to our house with almost no warning.

To completely understand the humor of this, you must know two things about me—I am certainly *not* a country girl who likes caring for animals, and I absolutely *am* a person who likes predictability and planning. So, when my darling husband told me we would be raising chickens, and eighteen chicks would be living in a box in our living room for several weeks, it was something that made me gasp outwardly and tense inwardly.

If I had told the story, I would have talked about how taxing this whole situation was for me or how nervous I was about caring for the baby chicks. I would have recounted how annoying the mess and the smell were and what a pain it was to clean out their box every week.

However, my sister talked about something entirely different. She shared how cute it was that I immediately became a mamma to those fuzzy chicks. She described the memory of watching me quickly become fully invested in those little ones. I researched how to nurture them during the first few weeks of life, paid close attention to their health, and even fed one of the babies with a medicine dropper when it was sick. Janna revealed how she admired the way I handled the whole situation despite how she knew it was absolutely not something I would have chosen of my own free will.

When I heard her perspective on the situation, it surprised me. As I was experiencing the circumstance, it felt burdensome, unnatural, and stressful. From my sister's point of view, it was a beautiful moment of grace and tenderness in my life. Hearing her say that was so uplifting. We cannot see ourselves from another's perspective unless the insight is shared with us. Therefore, it is essential for us to communicate all the good things we notice in each other's lives.

If we have a tough time recognizing wonderful qualities in ourselves, we must also realize other women struggle to see their own talents, gifts, and strengths. When we notice a lovely woman who always wears the perfect outfit, it is easy to think she knows how good she looks. But does she? The reality may be she does not feel pretty at all. We believe a person who has a fantastic singing voice is aware of her talent, but that may not be the case. A woman at church known for being a leader may have no clue the impact she has on others. A mom who is doing a great job rearing her children may only be feeling exhausted and ineffective.

Occasionally, a mature woman with a healthy level of self-esteem may have a reasonably accurate perception of her strengths and weaknesses. However, in my experience, we are too critical of ourselves, so we are way off when we try to discern how others view us.

Here is a challenge—find a woman who looks like she has it all together and compliment her in a profoundly personal way. You might be surprised that she has never thought of herself that way or struggles to believe such things about herself. Your comment might even bring tears to her eyes. More often than not, we do not hear kind words enough, and we are desperate to hear positive, uplifting ones more often.

I encourage you to not only say these words of encouragement to your fellow Sisters but actually write them down. Our memories fade over the years, and we forget those sweet words our friends have said to us. Then when Satan attacks, it is much harder to retrieve those memories and combat his condemnation. A written letter or card can be kept forever. Then your Sister can pull it out and read it whenever she is discouraged. Keep your own mementos in a special box or drawer to read again when you need some inspiration.

> *It does not take special writing skills to minister to someone through words... The most important thing is to continue abiding in Christ and reading His powerful words to you.*

Write to your Sisters in Christ often, telling them how you see God's handiwork in their lives and give them encouragement that can minister to them for years to come.

Actually accomplishing this might seem easier said than done. Some people may argue they are not good writers, and they do not know what to say. I promise you; it does not take special writing skills to minister to someone through words. So what does it require?

The most important thing is to continue abiding in Christ and reading His powerful words to you. The more you learn about Him, the more you see others through His eyes. Pray for God to give you the words to say, and He will fill you with His words.

Tell your Sister in Christ how you see God working in her life. Affirm a choice she has made to follow the Lord's will in a specific area. Encourage her in an endeavor that may be outside of her comfort zone. Describe how you see her transforming her own environment by sharing God with the people she is around. Tell her that her smile and friendliness are such an inspiration to you. Compliment her strength, patience, or perseverance in enduring a trying situation. Or simply thank her for being an encouragement to you in your life.

You do not have to be creative or inventive. Repeat God's Word right back to your friend. Psalm 149:4 says that "the Lord delights in his people," so tell your Sister that you delight in her. In 2 Corinthians 5:17, we are told that "if anyone is in Christ, he is a new creation. The old has passed away; behold the new has come" (ESV). Tell your friend about the new creation you see her becoming. God's words are powerful. Simply writing scripture to your Sister in Christ is enough.

Prayer is a great encourager, too. Tell your friend how you are specifically lifting her up to the Father through prayer. I have been on both the giving and receiving end of this, and it never fails to be a blessing.

At a meeting, I noticed a woman who seemed unhappy. I greeted her and asked how she was doing. She said she had recently had surgery and was tired. But something told me there was a deeper problem. God kept bringing her to my mind throughout the night and into the next day. In the past, I had let those moments slip away or quickly said a silent prayer for the person. That time, I made a point to do something more "sisterly." I decided to send her an email. Knowing so little about this woman or her situation, I had difficulty thinking about what to say. So, I told her she had been on my mind, and I had prayed this prayer for her:

Father, I lift up my Sister to you.
Please comfort her, heal her, and give her rest.
Help her know how loved and valued she is.
Help her see herself through Your eyes,
as Your precious daughter, highly favored.
Only You know her heart and what she needs.
I ask that you bless her and provide for her needs.
Amen.

I ended the email by asking her to let me know if I could do anything for her. Surprisingly, she opened up and revealed some very personal struggles she was experiencing. I was thankful she had been willing to share more with me because it gave me more specific ways to pray and minister to her.

The simple act of writing out my prayer and sending it to my Sister in Christ not only blessed her tremendously but also helped me connect with her more deeply.

When you minister to your Sister through your words, you are helping her experience God's love. The power is not in the exact words you choose; the power is in the act of sharing God with your Sister. Proverbs 16:24 says, "Kind words are like honey—sweet to the soul and healthy to the body," and Proverbs 18:4 states, "A person's words can be life-giving water; words of true wisdom are as refreshing as a bubbling brook." When you speak or write beautiful, life-giving words to your friend, you are uplifting her and glorifying God. There is no way this can fall short, no possible way it will fail to bless both you and her.

The power is not in the exact words you choose; the power is in the act of sharing God with your Sister.

We all hear voices in our heads. Some of us hear voices of condemnation. Some hear voices of temptation. I often hear the voice of my family's encouragement as I walk through life. When I need wisdom or motivation, their words echo in my mind. My thoughts are filled with years of memories of reading their sweet cards and hearing them spur me on, making it much easier to drown out the negative voices that vie for my attention.

What voices do you hear? Have you been given so many positive words of encouragement that your head is full of beautiful thoughts?

Or have you been bombarded with so much negativity that you wrestle with discerning the difference between the Spirit's conviction and the Enemy's condemnation?

My hope is that you hear the voice of Jesus in your mind, whispering kindness, love, and gentle guidance to you every day. I pray your Sisters in Christ are the Lord's voice in your life and that you make an effort to be the

Words of Encouragement

same encouraging voice in the lives of your Sisters.

Dear Sister, you have more of an impact on others than you realize. With only a few words, you can build someone up in their faith, give a friend hope in a desperate situation, open a woman's eyes to the beauty she has inside, and point a Sister toward Christ.

You do not have to be a gifted writer for your writing to be a gift. After all, God is the ultimate author of all things good and beautiful. So, bless your Sister by letting God's encouragement flow from your fingers and your mouth, and I promise you will reap precious blessings as well.

Reflection Questions

1. Do you find it easy or hard to give other women words of encouragement? Why do you think this is? If you struggle, how can you work on this skill? If this is easy for you, is there any way you could use this gift more often or more specifically?

2. What words of encouragement do you need to hear from a Sister in Christ today? What do you wish someone would say to you? Ask God to speak to your heart in this area.

3. Is there a woman in your life you could uplift with your words this week? Make a specific plan for how you can minister to her.

> *Kind words are like honey—sweet to the soul and healthy to the body.*
>
> *Proverbs 16:24*

> *A person's words can be life-giving water; words of true wisdom are as refreshing as a bubbling brook.*
>
> *Proverbs 18:4*

Chapter 7

Let Your Sisters Help

*Friendship is an opportunity to act on God's
behalf in the lives of the people that we're
close to, reminding each other who God is.*
—Shauna Niequist

My sisters and I loved to play games as children. From the early favorites of *Candy Land* and *Chutes and Ladders* to the later childhood games of *Yahtzee*, *Sorry*, and *Clue*, we had stacks of games in our closet. One of our absolute favorites was *Monopoly*. We could play for hours. Of course, part of that was because of our merciful manner of game-playing. When one person was about to declare bankruptcy, the other sister would graciously offer a generous deal to keep her in the game.

Growing up with this very gentle version of competition, it was quite an unnerving experience the first time I played *Monopoly* with my husband. He played to win—with no mercy. After my first few games with him, I learned to genuinely appreciate my sisters' more relaxed approach.

As the youngest of the four, I always looked forward to playtime with my sisters. I was saddened when they got older and had less desire for toys and games. I had the choice of sitting and doing more "grown-up" things or playing by myself. Being an introvert, I often chose to be alone.

When you play alone, you sometimes must be more creative in your approach, so I would find ways to play board games by myself, including *Monopoly*. You may wonder, "How do you do this by yourself?" Well, it involves make-believe and a deep sense of rule-following. For one player, I acted as myself and followed a strict approach for how I would make decisions. As the other player, I pretended to be Denise and did my best to imitate her typical strategy. It is amazing what one can do with enough boredom and determination!

All these moments of playing by myself gave me confidence in being alone and a sense of independence. These are valuable characteristics…sometimes. Then you wake up one day and realize you do not know how to ask for help or show that you need anybody. Independence can be quite lonely.

Sometimes one of the hardest things for me to do is admit I need someone else's help. Generally, I am the type of person who feels I can accomplish almost anything on my own if I give enough effort. As a child, I saw my mother raise four children, teach elementary school, and fill the stressful role of a preacher's wife while always somehow managing to cook dinner, clean house, and hand-make items for special occasions, like Smurf hats for every guest at my 6-year-old birthday party. So, when I became a mother, I naturally expected I would be exactly like her…Super Mom! Most of us have a person like this in our lives who seems like she can do it all, and we look at ourselves and ask, "If she does it, why can't I?"

One day, after expressing regret over not taking my children to the park enough, reading to them enough, or baking cookies with them enough, my mother sat me down and comforted me. She reminded me that every woman's life is unique; we all have different circumstances. More importantly, God gave every woman a special set of gifts. He equips us for what He wants us to accomplish, not for what we think we *should* accomplish. She reminded me I am not alone, and it is okay to ask others for help.

When we talk about what it means to be a great Sister in Christ, we primarily focus on what we must give and the service we should provide other women. Like many of you, I often start my day with a list of things I must do for my family, church, school, or others. I pray God will open my eyes to ways I should serve each day and how I can better show His love in my friendships. As I grow in my relationship with the Lord, those opportunities for ministry, service, and love are becoming more evident.

But most women do not need another thing on their

to-do list. Often what we wrestle with more than serving others is allowing others the opportunity to serve us. It reminds me of an illustration I have heard told many times.

A man is caught in a flood and is stranded, sitting on his roof surrounded by floodwaters. He prays to God to save him. Three different times someone comes along to rescue him—a rowboat, a motorboat, and a helicopter. Every time, the man refuses assistance, saying that God is going to save him. Finally, the man dies and, in heaven, asks God why He did not rescue him. God says, "I sent help three times. What more did you expect?"

Many of us will sit at home in tears over the difficulties we have faced that day, and we will cry out to God for relief. The next day, when a friend at church asks us how we are doing, we will say, "I'm fine, thanks." Like the man in the flood, we motion people along, acting like we are all okay. Maybe somewhere in our mind, we think God will send help in a more obvious way. We fail to see Jesus standing right before us offering a helping hand through our Sister in Christ, and we overlook the blessing God had prepared for us.

For me, it took great hardship to finally learn the humbling beauty of receiving without having anything to give in return. In 2009, our family went through an extraordinarily challenging time. This was right after we adopted our third child, Elizabeth. About a month after we welcomed her into our home, my husband and I decided I needed to return to work to help out financially.

In August, I started my new job teaching seventh-grade math, a grade level I had never taught before. In addition, I was writing the thesis for my master's degree in education. Life was notably busy.

Then, during the first few weeks of school, our whole world was turned upside down when our house caught fire in the middle of the night. I will never forget waking to the smell of hamburgers on the grill, wondering who was cooking. (We found out later we had accidentally left the grill on that night after we had made hamburgers.) Almost immediately, I heard the shattering of glass and jumped out of bed to investigate the noise, thinking my son was out of bed.

When I rounded the corner into my living room, all I saw was a blazing fire outside the broken window. Smoke billowed in from the back porch, and I screamed, "Fire!" During the next few minutes, Casey and I scrambled to get all three kids out of the house. By the time we carried the last child out, the house was filled with smoke and flames. We safely escaped just in time, and then we all stood on the lawn in our pajamas, watching our house burn.

Side note: it is advisable to wear yard-appropriate clothing to bed, just in case you find yourself suddenly needing to exit your home in an emergency. Unfortunately, I learned this lesson a little too late and stood that morning in our yard in only a t-shirt and scanty underwear. Fortunately, a neighbor noticed my dilemma and quickly brought me some shorts!

As we were standing there waiting for the fire trucks to arrive, bewildered and struggling to grasp what was happening, my five-year-old saw the blaze scorching his room. He gasped, "My toys!" It was a devastating loss that took us years to recover from.

So, you can imagine, with a new job, financial strains, two small children and an infant, graduate school, and now the loss of our home, life was extremely stressful.

To add to these trying circumstances, I had to function as a single mom while my husband was out of town for about a month. Every morning, I woke up at about 4:30 am to start the process of getting myself and the kids ready for the day. After a stop at daycare and a kindergarten drop-off, I had just enough time to make it to work. I spent the day adapting to my new job. Then I left school and made the rounds to pick up the children while trying to figure out something for dinner.

My evenings were spent chasing the little ones, washing dishes (by hand!), and helping my kindergartener with his homework. When they were finally tucked into bed, I stayed up late grading papers and planning the next day's lesson. Whenever a moment of extra time could be found, I worked on my graduate thesis. The next morning's alarm clock woke me up to do it all over again.

And those were the regular days.

There were weeks sprinkled in when every kid had the swine flu, or I was tackling a new financial crisis sparked by our house fire.

For the first time in my life, I reached the point where

I actually could not do it all by myself. I was forced to accept whatever aid I could, whether it was money, food, childcare, or even physical assistance. My brother-in-law provided the rental house we moved into right after the fire, and various people from our church donated every bit of the furniture. They searched their storage buildings and garages and brought us anything they could spare. One sweet lady from our church rescued some of the items from our house's wreckage and cleaned them for us.

At this time, we lived about three hours away from my sisters and parents, so my family took turns visiting me each weekend. They cleaned my house, watched our kids, and gave me a chance to rest. My husband's family was also a constant source of aid, providing money, helping hands, childcare, and so much more. Many people gave to us in so many ways that I couldn't even keep up with all the thank you notes I needed to write.

The hardest thing was knowing there was no way I could repay all that had been given to us. We could not do anything for anybody else during this period; all we could do was receive the blessings of other people's kindness.

That experience opened my eyes to see all the love God wants to show me. He wants to send me help and comfort, but I have to be willing to receive it. He desires to provide for me, but I must have the humility to accept His provision. Since that time, I cannot say it is always easy to accept other's service. However, God continues to teach me and show my heart the beauty that comes with laying my burdens at someone else's feet.

During the beginning of the COVID pandemic of 2020, my youngest son started having terrible digestive problems, resulting in trips to the emergency room and then to the hospital for a colonoscopy and endoscopy. After a few months of living in crisis and not knowing what was wrong with him, James was finally diagnosed with ulcerative colitis. It was a heartbreaking diagnosis because we knew this was not going away; it was a lifetime disease that would mean many changes in our diet and medicines.

Often, the way God eases our burden and provides rest is through the service of others.

On one of our first days home from the hospital, a friend from church asked if she could organize meals for us. My first inclination was to turn her down. I thought, "My legs aren't broken. I'm not sick. I actually can walk into the kitchen and cook food for my family right now. I'm sure other people have bigger needs than I do." Then God gently smacked me on the head and said, "Jennifer, sweet daughter, give yourself a break. You need to rest and focus on James. Let me help you. You don't need to be strong. I will be your strength."

The scripture from Matthew 11:28 came to mind. "Come to me, all you who are weary and burdened, and I will give you rest" (NIV). Often, the way God eases our burden and provides that rest is through the service of others. So, I texted my friend back and told her I would love to have meals provided. I admitted to her I am not a great cook, and one of my biggest challenges was preparing healthy food that satisfied my son's specific dietary needs. Several people made meals for us that were both tasty and healthy. This gave me the time to learn more about James's diagnosis, research recipes, and make a new meal plan for our family.

Though I felt kind of spoiled to have people bringing us meals, I was so grateful to have the extra time to adjust to my son's new needs. In the end, my sweet friend thanked *me* for allowing her to help. She said it was a blessing to be involved in our lives!

When we allow our Sisters to serve us, we provide them the opportunity to follow God's calling in their own lives.

Dear Sisters in Christ, we all need to give ourselves permission to receive the gifts God presents to us. We all know the delight we experience from loving others, but we also receive joy, hope, and peace when we willingly accept others' unconditional love. When we allow our Sisters to serve us, we provide them the opportunity to follow God's calling in their own lives. We offer them an avenue for intimacy with us that can never be fully achieved when we do not make ourselves vulnerable and humble.

It is not necessary for you to be on the brink of exhaustion or going through a crisis for you to ask for help. It could simply be you are having a rough day. We are terrible about comparing ourselves to other women and diminishing our everyday needs because we believe they pale in comparison to someone else's. God did not say, "Come to me, all you who have a really legitimate reason to be weary," or "I will give rest to the ones of you who deserve it the most." He wants us *all* to come and receive His blessings.

In fact, I'll go further in saying that hiding our needs from each other is more hurtful than helpful. It saddens me when I find out a friend has been in need, and I had not been given the opportunity to help. Somewhere in our heads, we think others will breathe a sigh of relief if they don't have to be involved—that somehow, we are sparing other women from the difficulty of serving us. But when we do not allow others to share in our burdens, we build higher and higher walls between us.

When you finally learn that someone right in front of you has been living in need of something, whether emotional or physical, it deepens a sense of isolation and loneliness. It is as if she has pulled away from you and is choosing to keep you at a distance, instead of letting you into her life.

If you are unwilling to ask for help until you are absolutely desperate, then by example, you are telling all the women around you they need to be in that same desperate place before they ask you for help. Yes, we need to check our motives and make sure we are not just playing the victim all the time. We also need to stop trying to be the rock all the time and allow Jesus to minister to us through our Sisters in Christ.

The other day a friend texted me and asked me to watch her daughter for a short while. As I got ready to go to her house that morning, I thought about how this situation usually plays out in our minds differently than what happens in reality.

When I ask others to help me, I typically feel apprehensive about inconveniencing them too much. I try to use their assistance as little as possible and worry about "putting them out," and I often wish I did not need their aid. In my head, I guess I think the other person wishes they did not have to help me either. That was not what was in my head that morning as I prepared to go to my friend's house. I was not burdened but rather happy and honored to assist her. I was excited to be invited into her life. I was overjoyed to be able to serve her.

Sometimes I see my friends, hear their frustrations and burdens, and wonder how I can do anything to make it better. This specific friend had been keeping a foster child and was struggling to cope with all that was related to this toddler's care, including various therapies and mediation visits to discuss termination of parental rights. For the most part, there was nothing I could do to ease her particular situation besides praying; I did that often. But

God was stirring my heart to serve her in more practical ways. What did she need from me? How could I bless her?

When she called to ask me to watch her child while she prepared for a garage sale, it felt so good to be able to ease her burden, even in that small way. In addition, we had an opportunity to talk and become closer. I am so thankful this friend gave me the chance to serve her and be part of her life. A slight shift in our perspective allows us to realize that asking others for help is not a weakness but rather a symbol of our willingness to be vulnerable and intimate with others.

I must confess how much of an issue this is for me. On the morning I wrote this chapter, I woke up with severe back pain. It hurt so bad I laid down on the couch and couldn't get up. I had to slowly roll myself onto my side just to get off the couch and onto my feet. Then I made breakfast for my family while doubled over in pain. Everyone else was still asleep, so I agonized in silence, not wanting to trouble anyone for assistance.

Later that day, when I continued writing this chapter, it struck me how easy it is to *say* we should ask for help but how tough it is to *actually* do it.

After this needed reminder, when my mother-in-law offered to cook dinner for us that night, I accepted.

The biggest obstacle to allowing others to serve us is often our own pride. A healthy dose of pride allows us to see our own value and worth as a daughter of God. However, sometimes we let pride break past this healthy boundary. We say we are "fine" when we really are not.

We push away helping hands we actually need. We take on tasks we really shouldn't do.

The biggest obstacle to allowing others to serve us is often our own pride.

When I looked back at the reason my back was hurting, it was all because of pride. A few days before, I had been at another woman's house for a fine arts enrichment day with other homeschool families. I arrived early and saw she needed assistance rearranging the living room for the event. So, I jumped in and started moving furniture around.

For some women, moving a few tables and chairs might be no big deal. But for me, it's a big no-no. I have a particular type of back problem that means any heavy lifting will ensure a few days of severe lower back pain. I tend to ignore this limitation in my life and act like I can do anything.

I didn't want to appear lazy.

I didn't want to admit a weakness.

So, when I saw her need, instead of being honest about my back issues and saying, "No," I hid my limitation and moved furniture anyway. My pride resulted in three days of pain and me having to ask for help at home.

The scripture 2 Corinthians 12:9 says, "'My grace is all you need. My power works best in weakness.' So now I am glad to boast about my weaknesses, so that the power of Christ can work through me."

When we ask for help or simply admit we cannot serve someone else at the moment, we are not being lazy, whiny, or selfish. We are recognizing an important truth—we need others, and more than anything, we need Christ's power in our lives. When we admit our weaknesses, we open ourselves to the possibility of receiving the most significant gifts.

Friends should participate in each other's joys *and* burdens as they journey together in their walk of faith. God did not design us to be independent but rather dependent. We need each other, and we need Him. When we honestly admit this and share it with other women, it frees us, brings intimacy in our relationships, and ultimately moves us toward stronger dependence on Jesus.

When we admit our weaknesses, we open ourselves to the possibility of receiving the most significant gifts.

Dear Sister, stop trying to do it all, endure it all, and fix it all by yourself, and let your Sisters share Christ's love with you through service. Allow God to take care of you personally by letting other women be His hands and feet. Ladies, I pray we all have the grace and humility to let our

Sisters serve and love us in ways we can never repay, for that is one of the beautiful ways we experience God and His love for us.

Reflection Questions

1. Do you allow others to help you? If not, what is hindering this? If so, reflect on the mindset you have that makes this more comfortable for you.

2. Currently, do you need a friend's support but are unwilling or afraid to ask for it? Think about the source of this fear and how you can overcome it.

3. Is there someone you know that needs a gentle nudge regarding this concept? How can you encourage a friend to feel more comfortable asking for help?

But he said to me, "My grace is sufficient for you, for my power is made perfect in weakness."

2 Corinthians 12:9 (NIV)

Come to me, all you who are weary and burdened, and I will give you rest.

Matthew 11:28

Chapter 8

Show Me Jesus

*Real, connected, intimate time with Jesus
is the very thing that grows our faith, shifts
our minds, brings about revival in our souls,
and spreads to others.*
—Jennie Allen

In my opinion, flowers are one of God's most beautiful creations. If I am in a depressed mood, even a small bouquet of flowers sitting on my kitchen table can brighten my day. I am amazed at how God made each one completely unique but equally lovely. From roses to wildflowers, I enjoy every variety, but one of my favorites is the sunflower. It is so cheerful and stands tall and bold wherever it grows, but the thing I love most is how it follows the sun across the sky.

To me, a sunflower represents the type of dependence we should have on Christ. Our face should always be pointed toward the only Son, following Him throughout the day, looking to Him for our sustenance, ever thankful for the life-giving light He provides.

I think of my sisters as sunflowers. There have been so many times over the years when I have lacked faith, struggled to see God, or had a hard time navigating through a particular trial—when I was not sure which way to look. But I could look at my sisters, see them pointing toward God with their kind words, gentle wisdom, and consistent hope, and my own face would be directed to the Son above. I believe this is one of the most essential purposes of a Sister in Christ—to point us to Jesus!

Our face should always be pointed toward the only Son, following Him throughout the day, looking to Him for our sustenance, ever thankful for the life-giving light He provides.

I am so blessed to be surrounded by women who can give me perspective and guide me in my walk with the Lord. They are the instrument God often uses to speak into my life. He whispers to me through their words, and He draws me close to Him through their gentle nudging. Too easily, I find myself wandering off course, wrestling with faith, or wavering in my conviction. Fortunately, my Sisters in Christ are often there to pull me back on course and give me a renewed spirit.

One Saturday morning, my sisters and I joined each other for coffee at Mom's house, as we had done so many times before. Everyone took turns sharing various happenings in their lives. I do not remember everything we talked about that day. Some days we keep it light and discuss topics such as decorating or funny children stories. Other days we problem-solve a crisis. Whatever the subject that day, my sisters noticed throughout our conversation that I was not my usual self. Finally, they prodded, and I revealed what was troubling me.

I felt an overwhelming burden that I had to take care of everyone in my life and didn't feel I could have a rest. I shared with them about when I had laid my head down for a few minutes to take a nap, and my young son James had run out in the street.

I explained how I was not sleeping well because I had James sleep on a pallet in my room every night. He had been having seizures and recently had been care-flighted to a children's hospital in Dallas after a series of three life-threatening ones. The doctors gave us CPR lessons and emergency medicine to administer if his seizure lasted too long. Honestly, instead of comforting me, all this information only stressed me out even more. It made it all-too-real how serious his condition was and added pressure that I might actually have to use these tools.

What if I didn't remember how to do it? What if I did it incorrectly? What if I was not there when he had a seizure?

In addition to the concerns related to James's seizures, my kids were all relatively young and needy, and I was just starting my homeschooling journey. Knowing the education of my kids rested solely on my shoulders made it a daunting task.

From my perspective, I was a woman treading water while trying to hold everyone else's head above the surface. If I took a moment of a break, it felt as if they would all sink. I was physically and emotionally exhausted.

My sisters listened and comforted me. Then, in a very clarifying moment, Denise said, "Jennifer, you're forgetting one significant thing—God. When you took a nap, God protected your son from getting hurt in the street. Even when James stopped breathing during his seizures, God kept him alive." She continued on, reminding me that ultimately, I am not the one who protects my family anyway; it is God. I had not realized I was inflating my own importance while failing to recognize God's incredible power and protection in my life. Along with all my sisters and Mom, Denise spoke God's truth to me in a powerful way. They reminded me of who God is and who I am as His daughter. Amazingly, I slept remarkably well that night, having a burden lifted from me.

You see, when I opened my heart, I received an immeasurable blessing—the gift of God speaking to me through my sisters. Even more importantly, when they talked to me, they spoke truth. They spoke from God's word and pointed me back to Him. Everything they said was focused on helping me have a deeper relationship with Christ and seeing His hand in my life.

They didn't say, "Oh, poor darling. You just need to

hire a babysitter and have your husband help out more." They also didn't say, "Well, this is how life is when you are married and have small children. This stage will pass eventually." My sisters did not advise me to research more about seizures and CPR so I would be well-equipped to handle any situation that arose. My mother did not hand me a list of resources to guide me in homeschooling. Though this advice would have been useful at some point, it was not what I needed at the time.

My family had the wisdom to recognize that the real battle I was fighting was not practical in nature but rather spiritual. I did not need a solution; I needed hope and faith to carry me through my journey. Practical suggestions and "you can do it" mantras might have given me immediate relief, but they would not have served to strengthen my faith and help me rest in God. My sisters knew that, more than anything, I needed Christ!

We need our Sisters in Christ to give us practical advice, but we also need them to provide more than that. We need our Sisters to share the Lord with us in a personal and intimate way.

Anyone can give us cooking advice, tell us where to find a great discount on a needed item, or point us to a website with fantastic household cleaning tips. We have so many resources at our fingertips that can help us find solutions to many of our day-by-day struggles. Yet, those superficial fixes and life hacks will only take us so far. They may help us with an immediate problem, but they will not heal our broken hearts, give us strength in unbearable situations, or help us fully understand the love of Christ.

Our Sister in Christ relationships need to be deeper and more purposeful than the relationships we have with the non-Christians or acquaintances in our lives. If we keep our Christian relationships at the same casual level as our other relationships, then we miss out on so much. If our only solution to a friend's problem is to provide an online resource, book, or practical tip, then we are overlooking opportunities to share our faith and grow deeper, more powerful relationships.

In some situations, it can be uncomfortable to be bold about our faith. We do not want to seem preachy or self-righteous or make someone feel like we are judging them. Or maybe we think we are sharing a truth we believe our Sister in Christ already knows. We suppose, "Surely she doesn't need me to tell her that," as we convince ourselves to hold back something that seems so apparent to us.

However, God calls us all to be a witness for Him, and we must be bold and wise in carrying out this mission. This calling is not meant for only reaching the lost or in specific circumstances; it is for every occasion and everyone we meet.

If you are anything like me, you need to be told over and over again some of the simple truths of God's love and mercy before they will ultimately take root in your life. We should never underestimate how much our Sisters need us to share our faith and wisdom with them, even if it seems like nothing new or ground-breaking. Even a faithful, strong, veteran Christian may occasionally need you to point her to Christ! We all struggle with different aspects of our walk with Jesus, and we all need someone bold enough to guide us, encourage us, and minister to us.

We should never underestimate how much our Sisters need us to share our faith and wisdom with them, even if it seems like nothing new or ground-breaking.

It takes practice and intentionality to learn how to do this well, with love and humility. This is a skill I am still working on, but my sisters have mastered it. They are great at speaking truth with wisely chosen words and humility, in a way that allows you to see they are still learning themselves. You can see the love in their eyes and hear it in their voices. When they cut through all the nonsense of the world and direct me pointedly to Christ, the power of the Holy Spirit is evident, and it touches my heart more than any earthly wisdom could.

Ladies, we often have so much to say to each other and are full of advice. We must be careful that our words and guidance are wholly focused on directing our Sisters to God and showing His love, power, and grace in our lives. The advice we give to others testifies to what is in our hearts and indicates where our wisdom comes from.

If I find myself mostly quoting memes and movie one-liners, I must ask myself if I am filling myself too much with worldly wisdom and not enough with God's Word. Don't get me wrong; I love a good meme as much as anyone, and I delight in all the cute quotes and stories I read online. There is a time and a place for all of this. But if the wisdom I impart to other ladies is mostly repeating the world's view of life and not pointing others to God, then it is time to rethink my message.

Though it is definitely critical to express our faith and wisdom with humility and gentleness, it is also the receiver's responsibility to have the appropriate attitude. When our Sisters in Christ take that bold leap and offer wisdom, advice, or share their faith, we must receive their words with an open mind and heart. When our friends try to help us along our path, they are not always going to choose the perfect words, have the best timing, or provide the greatest solution. Even when they are well-intentioned, our Sisters might come across in a negative way or simply struggle to communicate effectively. We are all learning and growing in our faith together. So, we must always choose grace and believe the best in our Sisters.

When we seek out wisdom from other women, we need to be ready to listen with an open heart and allow ourselves to hear God's message in the voice of our Sisters. I do not go to my Sisters to merely rubber-stamp my own beliefs. I expect honesty from them, even if it hurts a little. I must be willing to accept that I am wrong or misguided. I can choose to be offended by the Truth or decide to let the Holy Spirit have a chance to change me.

Over the years, I have been so thankful for the wise counsel of my sisters. When I feel beaten down by someone's unkind words, they remind me of my true identity in Christ. When I am overwhelmed by my responsibilities, they help me recall how God has equipped me beyond measure for all the tasks He has given me. When I am having a difficult time making a decision or when I am encountering a huge obstacle, they ask me if I have sought the Lord's wisdom. When I am exhausted and losing my resolve, they share God's Word with me, "Let us not become weary in doing good, for at the proper time we will reap a harvest if we do not give up" (Galatians 6:9 NIV). When I have a bad attitude about something, they have also given me a gentle kick in the pants.

No matter the situation, they respond with truth, love, kindness, wisdom, and grace.

As I ponder this concept of encouraging others by pointing them to Christ, it makes me think about *The Wizard of Oz*. Yes, I know that is a little odd. After all, it is just a children's story.

Dorothy is a simple girl, with no special gifts or talents. Her particular desire is to find the only one who can fulfill her need—the Great and Powerful Oz. Along the way, she meets three others seeking to fill their own needs—a tin man, a cowardly lion, and a scarecrow. Dorothy cannot solve their problems, but she is confident she knows someone who can. She offers them hope, telling them that the one she seeks will be able to meet their needs too. Arm in arm, they set out on their quest.

On their journey, the Wicked Witch of the West torments Dorthy and her friends with various obstacles to keep them from the Great and Powerful Oz. Dorothy is not dissuaded. With focused determination and hope, she pushes forward. And when one of them is threatened, the others fight to save them.

When I watch the story of *The Wizard of Oz*, I see the beautiful testimony of an ordinary girl, just like me. In my opinion, Dorothy is an example of the type of Sister in Christ we should all strive to be. When the Enemy's tactics are used to torment our friends, we can help make a difference by leading them to the One who can satisfy all their needs[6].

You may feel ill-equipped to be this type of Christian leader for another woman. Maybe you are younger or a new Christian. You might believe you have nothing to offer or feel inadequate. But you do not have to be the most experienced, most well-versed in the Bible, or most talented to minister to your fellow Sisters. You do not have to have all the answers or be a perfect example of Christian virtues.

Only one thing is required to point others to Christ—you must know the One you seek, Christ Himself!

If you are seeking Him daily, then you can help others seek Him.

If you are reading His Word, then you can share His Word with your friend.

If you are reaching out to Him in prayer and asking for His Spirit to guide you, then He will give you wisdom and point you in the right direction.

Only one thing is required to point others to Christ— you must know the One you seek, Christ Himself!

As Sisters in Christ, we must look to each other for help along the road of life, because the journey is rough sometimes. When given an opportunity to share advice, we have a choice of meeting that need with a superficial, temporary, or worldly fix or offering something of substance, the type of wisdom and healing only God can provide.

So, the next time a Sister expresses difficulty in parenting, hand her that excellent parenting book, but don't stop there. Meet her deeper need by gently reminding her how God is there to guide and equip her if only she seeks Him. When a friend explains how she is so busy she barely has time to cook, give her that quick and easy crockpot recipe, but then point her to God's Word and the rest He so desperately wants her to have.

A friend of mine unexpectedly offered me spiritual comfort at a time when I was suffering physically. While I was recovering from surgery, she brought me a meal. Before she left, she asked if she could pray with me. Many people have brought me meals over the years, but she is the only one who had ever stopped to pray with me. I am sure others had prayed privately for me, but this personal gesture was a surprising extra gift. She prayed a short, simple prayer, nothing elaborate or especially memorable in itself, but it left a significant impression on me. I really wasn't that close to this woman at the time, but I immediately felt more like I could trust and confide in her.

This moment reminds me how a very simple act can create an avenue for deeper relationships and also boldly point a friend to Christ. Taking a meal to a person is a great act of service. Praying with a Sister in her time of need is a sweet extra step that reminds both people of the importance of seeking Christ in all situations.

As we engage with our Sisters, we must be bold yet gentle, truthful yet compassionate, wise yet humble. We should do our best to respond to other women with God's truth instead of the world's wisdom and direct our friends to seek Christ, instead of asking Google. When we consistently remind each other of God's power and protection in our lives and point each other to Jesus in all things, the result will be better than anything we could ever imagine or accomplish in our own strength.

We must be the sunflower in each other's lives, always having our own face pointed toward Jesus and ever-so-gently directing our Sisters to the live-giving Son above.

Reflection Questions

1. Do you believe you spend an adequate amount of time studying God's Word and seeking His wisdom? What are ways you could improve in this area?

2. Think about your discussions with other women in your life...

   Do you shy away from speaking about God and your faith? If so, why?

   If not, reflect on how you developed your comfort with sharing your faith. How could you help your Sisters in Christ become more comfortable with this?

> *Sing to the Lord; praise his name. Each day proclaim the good news that he saves. Publish his glorious deeds among the nations. Tell everyone about the amazing things he does.*
>
> *Psalm 96:2-3*

> *In your hearts revere Christ as Lord. Always be prepared to give an answer to everyone who asks you to give the reason for the hope that you have. But do this with gentleness and respect.*
>
> *1 Peter 3:15 (NIV)*

Chapter 9

Embrace Your Differences

*Insecurity will rob us of some of the
richest woman-to-woman relationships
of our lives...turning potential friends
into competitors.*
—Beth Moore

Christmas has always been a favorite holiday. Like most kids, I loved the suspense of waiting to see what I would get. As I grew older, I began to enjoy giving gifts to others. One Christmas, Grandmother gave Denise and me money to do our own Christmas shopping. With cash in hand, and barely old enough to walk around the mall alone, we started off on our adventure. Denise and I were so excited to see what we could buy with $60!

Our oldest sister had just moved out of the house. We found a tiny ceramic cottage that was the perfect decoration for her new place. For our other sister, we chose a soft, pretty sweater. Next, we bought a small bottle of perfume for Mom. My sister and I were on a roll and delighted at our choices. It was time to buy the last present, but our smiles drooped when we counted our money. There were only a few dollars left to buy something for Dad. Not allowing our enthusiasm to be squashed, we marched into the next store with pride and walked out with a nice pair of black socks.

Later, when handing out these presents to our family, each person showed appreciation for their gift, even our dad. As adults, when we remember the disparity we felt over the plain socks we gave to Dad compared to the thoughtful gifts for Mom and our sisters, both Denise and I chuckle. As children, my sister and I were incredibly proud of ourselves for buying and giving Christmas presents with a loving attitude. They had been graciously received in that same spirit. Our dad never flinched when he opened his single pair of socks; he showed as much excitement as the others did with their gifts.

We girls are so thankful our parents showed such genuine acceptance of each of us, whatever the gifts we gave. I fully believe that is exactly how God sees each of us, daughters who are giving the best gifts they can. Oh, how I wish we Sisters in Christ could always see each other that the same way!

Sometimes I crave the simplicity of those days, and I desire to have a childlike perspective once again, untainted by the world's tendency toward comparison. Unfortunately, despite our parents' best efforts to avoid comparing us, I still found myself battling this habit as I grew up.

Since I am the baby of the family, I have spent much of my life comparing myself to my three older sisters. When I was in school, some of my teachers would ask, "Are you the sister of _____? You must be really smart. I bet you are a great student." The expectation of greatness was there before the year began because all three of my sisters were terrific students.

The rest of my life was no different. I found I even had expectations of myself just because we shared the same genetics. I assumed I would be the exact same type of parent, wife, homemaker, cook, decorator, and teacher they would be, and those expectations set me up for considerable disappointment. My life, in many ways, looks markedly different from theirs. I have had to learn over the years how to search only for God's expectations of me and live them out in the way he designed especially for me—not for them.

Even though I know how destructive comparison can be, I still manage to compare myself to others more often than I should. Over the years, I have found that measuring myself against other women leads to one of two things—defeat or self-importance. Either way, I fall short of God's desire for me.

If I decide I am second-rate to someone, I feel worthless, inadequate, and unimportant. When I mistakenly believe myself to be much better than others, I end up filled with unhealthy pride and arrogance. No matter which side of the fence I land upon, I find myself in a joyless pit, way off target from where God wants me to be.

As we journey through different seasons of life or interact with various people, we may find ourselves vacillating from one end of the spectrum to the other, moving from arrogance in one moment to complete shame or rejection in another. I have a lot of experience at both, so I feel it only honest to share a story about how both types of comparison have impacted me.

Measuring myself against other women leads to one of two things—defeat or self-importance. Either way, I fall short of God's desire for me.

When I was younger, I tended to land on the side of pride more often. I will never forget the moment when God opened my eyes to see the depth of my judgmental and prideful heart. I was attending a women's retreat in my early thirties.

During this time in my life, I was a woman who felt I had it all together. I knew what I believed, what I wanted, who I was, and who everyone else should be. I had not endured much hardship, a little here and there, and I was unsympathetic to others who could not "get their acts together." I did not see the value in women who were not like me. Though I was kind and easy to get along with on the outside, inside, I harbored unkind thoughts and considered myself better than many others I met.

God used those three days, surrounded by women from all different backgrounds, to gently show me how I needed to change my heart.

At the beginning of the weekend, we were assigned seats at round tables, and we were asked to keep those seats throughout the weekend. This provided the opportunity to come to know the ladies at our table more intimately. Inwardly, I groaned as I was seated next to a woman I felt was the complete opposite of me, and I struggled to connect with her. Her speech and dress were not at all like mine, and she expressed different interests and views of life. In my immaturity, I did not see the point in getting to know a woman with which I appeared to have nothing in common. Looking back, I do not doubt that this seating arrangement was divinely orchestrated!

Throughout the weekend, I encountered God and the women around me in a way that pierced the hard armor of my heart and challenged all my preconceived notions. I heard the testimonies of unlikely women who God used in incredible ways. I was served by ladies of all walks of life with a depth of love and genuine compassion, unlike anything I had ever experienced apart from my own family. Slowly, God helped me see women through His eyes, and He gently started softening my heart.

Then, it was time for the Lord's Supper. We were instructed to serve communion to the person on our left, and of course, the person on my left was this woman who

I was finding it difficult to love. I can still vividly remember how God almost instantly transformed my heart in that moment. As I served her the elements, I was overcome with genuine love for this woman who, only a few days before, had seemed unlovable to me. Even the way I perceived her appearance changed. Instead of seeing flaws in her face or hair, I noticed her warm smile and kind eyes.

As with all transformations, though there may be quick spurts of growth, the true lasting change happens over time. God spent several years working on this nasty part of my spirit. He slowly helped me change from a judgmental snob to a woman who genuinely cherishes all women and looks forward to learning about each one's unique story.

Experience is a great teacher, and the work the Holy Spirit did in my heart during the next decade of my life was immeasurable. I softened, I learned, I matured, and I grew in my relationship with Christ. As I started recognizing my own sinfulness, I became less prideful and more understanding of others.

Unfortunately, I did not stop comparing myself to other women. Satan found ways to use my new, more humble attitude to heighten my own insecurities. It is amazing how easily I sometimes landed on the other side of that fence, feeling inferior and of little value.

Years later, the comparison trap continued to steal my joy. My children were four, five, and nine years old. In addition to the normal, everyday parental struggles, extra challenges were added with a recent diagnosis of a rare genetic condition in my two youngest children. This altered gene caused them to be delayed in both cognitive and physical areas. When we adopted our children, we had no idea they had this chromosomal deletion. So, in addition to the sudden and unexpected adoptions, the news of extra challenges also threw us off balance. To add to our stress, no doctor had ever heard of this genetic condition or could give us any useful information regarding it.

During those early years, with such limited information, we had a hard time fully understanding and accepting our children's difficulties. To help you relate, it might be similar to finding out your child has autism or Down's Syndrome.

One of the biggest obstacles our children faced was communication skills, especially James. Even at five years old, he mainly used single words to tell us what he wanted, and even those were sometimes hard to understand. This created quite a bit of parenting strife, and he often got upset when we could not figure out what he wanted.

Around this time, my whole family (parents, sisters, and their families included) decided to vacation together in Tennessee. We had several struggles with the children on the trip. First, a hiking excursion presented extra physical challenges. My children required quite a bit of help and slowed our group down tremendously. It was clear from the beginning, my family was not able to keep up with the others.

While at the cabin, it felt as though all aspects of life were more difficult with our children. From helping them eat, dress, and potty to finding ability-appropriate activities to communicating with them about almost anything, Casey and I seemed to move from one frazzled moment to the next. Everything with our children took longer, required more intervention, and involved extra drama. From my perspective, my sisters' children were all easy to handle, self-sufficient, and well-behaved. Of course, they were all older, ranging from nine to eighteen years old, but that did not stop me from comparing my children to them.

During the whole vacation, I felt as though my parenting skills were being put on display for all to observe and analyze. Finally, one child's meltdown over something as simple as food put me over the edge.

After dealing with the situation, I went to the back porch and just cried. I felt as if I was an amateur parent among professionals, and I was floundering. My mom came to talk to me, and finally, we spoke with all my sisters.

They could have chosen to say so many things. Instead, they emphatically communicated one specific message to me—that they believe God specifically chose my husband and me as these children's parents, and God had uniquely equipped us to love, guide, and discipline them in the exact way they needed to be parented. They reminded me that any advice they gave was simply an attempt at being helpful. It was not a judgment or criticism. My family made it evident that they respected my husband and me as we parented our children. What powerful words I needed to hear!

I remember listening to a sermon about David and Goliath and knew God brought it to my attention at that exact time for a special purpose. When David was getting ready for battle against Goliath, Saul dressed him in his own tunic and gave him armor, a helmet, and a sword (1 Samuel 17:38-39). David tried walking around in Saul's battle gear, but he could not get used to them.

Here is the detail of the story I had not noticed before—he told Saul, "I cannot go in these," and took them off (v. 39). Instead, he gathered five stones and his sling. David had learned how to use a slingshot and stones long ago, and in his heart, he knew they were the right tools for him. It is with these weapons, not Saul's, that he slayed Goliath. God had prepared him for this battle and equipped him in his own way.

Saul, with his own wisdom about how one *should* approach a battle, had tried to equip David to face a giant. In fact, almost all of us would have done the same thing—handed David every bit of heavy armor and battle-worthy weapon we could find. However, *David* was the one chosen by God to battle the Philistines, not *Saul*. That means only David knew God's plan for him and how best to defeat the giant.

In the situation with my three kids, me attempting to parent the way my sisters parented and expecting the same results was like me trying to slay my giants with my sisters'

Embrace Your Differences

weapons and armor; it just was not going to work! I had to stop comparing myself and fully recognize the uniqueness of my situation. Then I had to lean into the Lord and look only to Him for wisdom. Nobody in my family had ever slain a giant like mine, and God had not chosen them for this task.

Now that my children are older, it is exciting to see how God has continued to empower, guide, and mold me as their parent. He has worked miracles with my children both through me and in spite of me, especially as I have continued to homeschool the two with special needs.

Some women have been called to have large families; others have been called to be single. Some women work in the mission field in a foreign country; others find their mission work in their own home or place of employment. Like me, many have chosen to teach their children at home, and others, frankly, would not even consider it. While we agree that our Heavenly Father directs all our paths according to His will, we must recognize that God does not set every woman on the same course. His plan for each individual person is as unique as David's battle against Goliath.

Still, it is remarkable how often women will subtly suggest that one person's path is not as ordained as another's. I have heard women say they don't see how a mom could put her child in daycare or work outside the home. I have seen women treat a single lady as someone who must not have anything to do all day because she does not have children to care for. I have listened as one woman explains to another why her specific situation is more challenging than someone else's. I have experienced having a woman tell me why I have faced a certain trial as if she personally knew God's thoughts and plans for me. When I went through infertility problems, people told me I would get pregnant as soon as I stopped trying, unwittingly suggesting that it was my own fault I was not getting pregnant.

Our job is not to critique or analyze but rather to stand in support of our Sister in Christ and cheer her on!

Often, we do not even realize how such quick, thoughtless comments can profoundly wound another woman and send the message that her challenge is not real, her chosen mission is not noble, or her choice is not God's will. We must be purposeful in conveying the opposite message—that we recognize God's individual call to a specific journey for each of our lives. Our job is not to critique or analyze but rather to stand in support of our Sister in Christ and cheer her on!

Think how differently my vacation could have turned out if my sisters had chosen to respond in judgment instead of gentleness. I already knew deep down that every individual was uniquely designed by God and had been given a special purpose. I understood that comparing myself to my sisters was ridiculous and pointless. However, knowing something in your head and letting that belief saturate your life can be a far distance away from each other.

While I spilled tears on the back porch after dealing with my child's breakdown, I needed to hear my sisters take this general belief in each woman's God-given purpose and make it personal and relevant to me, reminding me why I should not compare myself to anyone else. During this fragile moment on vacation, their words helped me internalize this belief and ultimately pointed me back to my Lord and His will for my life.

We all need to purposely let other women know we respect their relationship with God and the distinct way in which He leads each person. Just like in David's life, it is okay to give advice or offer armor and weapons for the battle. Just be careful to do it in such a way that lets the other woman know you still respect her even if she decides to throw off that armor and choose a different way.

Comparing ourselves to others invades almost every aspect of our lives. In fact, it sometimes even feels necessary, comfortable, just a natural part of existence. With Pinterest, Instagram, Facebook, and all the other online platforms, we can hardly escape the trap of comparison. But we must actively guard against it, or it will easily steal our joy.

Sometimes measuring yourself against others will lead you to feel "more highly of yourself than you ought" and cause you to overlook the beautiful gift in the Sister you have right in front of you (Romans 12:3). Other times, comparison will deflate you so much you wonder how God can use you for anything good.

If we all know deep down the detrimental impact of comparison, how do we stop ourselves from doing it? For me, the only way I can keep from comparing myself to others is by abiding in Christ and looking only to Him for guidance about who I am, what I should do, and where I am falling short.

Directly across from where I sit every morning, I have artwork displaying the scripture Proverbs 16:3. "Commit to the Lord whatever you do and He will establish your plans" (NIV). It is a constant reminder that He is the only one who is allowed to tell me what my plans should be or where my value lies. It also reminds me of my part. I must commit everything to Him—my hopes, dreams, goals, and to-do list. What I offer Him belongs to nobody else—not to my kids, husband, or society, only to Him. I must use discretion in listening to another's advice or critique and block out everything that does not fit closely with what He tells me.

If I look to anyone else for my vision or use any other standard besides His Word to judge how I am doing, then my perspective will be warped, my effectiveness will be hindered, and ultimately, I will stray from the path He wants me on.

Dear sweet sister, if God wanted us all to be the same, He would have made us all that way. When you focus less on how you compare to others and more on your Creator, you will find you start truly valuing, understanding, and cherishing every woman He created. God designed each woman with individual struggles, specific gifts, unique choices, and sometimes interesting and mysterious paths.

When you focus less on how you compare to others and more on your Creator, you will find you start truly valuing, understanding, and cherishing every woman He created.

As you spend more time with the Lord of the universe, you will be able to completely rest in the assurance of His genuine love. Then you will find it easier to stop reaching for purpose, fighting for position, searching for your value, struggling to get noticed, or pushing other people down below you. You are enough, and you are valuable because God made you in His image, and He is your maker. You are a reflection of God's glory. Like the colors in a rainbow, we are all different and yet perfectly reflect light from the same source.

Sisters, that also means that the woman who really irritates you, the Sister in Christ who offended you, and the friend who betrayed you—she is also enough, valuable, and made in God's image.

Let that sink in for a minute.

We can't fully embrace our own identity in Christ

unless we recognize that every other woman out there, even those who have hurt us, is also a daughter of God, deserving of the same grace and forgiveness we expect to receive ourselves.

My parents always told each one of us girls that we were their favorite daughter, and it was true. God feels the same way about each of us. We are all His favorites. We are different types of flowers, each one beautiful in her own way. When you put us all together, we form a fragrant bouquet, perfectly designed by God.

Let us not judge ourselves as either better or worse than any other woman but rather enjoy being one of His numerous favorites, a specially created flower in His garden.

We can't fully embrace our own identity in Christ unless we recognize that every other woman out there is also a daughter of God, deserving of the same grace and forgiveness we expect to receive ourselves.

Instead of noticing our differences, we must focus on all the wonderful things that unite us—our universal struggles, common goals, and most importantly, the One Lord and Savior who leads us all. Let's cherish all our Sisters' unique qualities, respect each other's individual paths, and relish the joy that comes from seeing others from God's perspective.

Reflection Questions

1. Do you find it hard to befriend women who are unlike you, or, in contrast, do you have an inspiring testimony to share about a friendship with a woman quite different from you?

2. Think about the circumstances that promote a tendency to compare. What are your own personal struggles in this area?

3. What specific preventive measures can you take to avoid the comparison trap?

> *Be completely humble and gentle; be patient, bearing with one another in love.*
>
> Ephesians 4:2 (NIV)

> *Don't think you are better than you really are. Be honest in your evaluation of yourselves, measuring yourselves by the faith God has given us.*
>
> Romans 12:3

Chapter 10

You Are Called to Be a Sister!

Do not waste time bothering whether you "love" your neighbor; act as if you did. As soon as we do this, we find one of the great secrets. When you are behaving as if you loved someone, you will presently come to love him.
—C. S. Lewis

Growing up, Denise and I acted a lot like twins. She was a year and a half older than me, but we were best friends. We shared a bedroom, wore matching clothes, and spent most of our time together. We played, danced, sang, made up stories, read to each other, and even worked together. We usually got along great. There were also times when we argued, hurt each other's feelings, or just did not want to be around each other.

When Denise and I were about seven and five years old, we recognized our relationship was not as loving as it had been previously. We spent less time playing together and more time being unkind to each other. Our family moved a lot during our youth. In our previous town, Kingsville, we had been much closer, more like best friends. So, Denise and I made a pact to try to rekindle the closeness we had there. We called this "Kingsville Rules."

Anytime one of us was being bratty or unkind, the other would say, "Kingsville Rules." This was the code word used to remind each other to act like best friends, even if our hearts were not feeling it. "Kingsville Rules" meant we must sit together in the same seat, instead of far apart, and we must share everything. If one of us wanted to play something and the other was not interested, saying "Kingsville Rules" would prompt us to find a way to play together, even if it meant giving up our own selfish desires.

Looking back, it was clear, even as children, we knew what being a sister was all about, and we longed for that deeper, sweeter kind of relationship. We recognized that our actions toward each other should not always depend on how we felt at the moment, and it was never acceptable to decide we did not want to be a sister that day. Instead, we needed to work hard on our relationship, make an effort to be close, spend time with each other, and do our best to put the other sister's interests above our own.

Our hearts knew when we were not treating each other the way we should, and we had to remind each other of that "something better" we desired. It is the same way now in adulthood. Our relationship is not perfect, but we hold that beautiful ideal in our hearts. Now, we may not exchange code words with each other when one of us is a little off track, but we do share God's Word and point each other to the true Ideal.

Being a Sister in Christ takes hard work and intentionality. A friendship formed from common interests and similar personalities may not require much effort, but the Sisters in your life are not always there by choice. God places women in our lives and calls us to be a Sister, even when this person seems so different. When you think about it, even biological sisters are frequently total opposites. Maybe that is a beautiful, purposeful blessing from God.

Janna and I are noticeably different. Janna graduated with an English and psychology degree while I majored in mathematics. She enjoys old black and white movies, and my favorite genre is psychological thrillers. I am married with three kids, and Janna is single. She loves decorating as a hobby; I think of it as a chore. Janna can read for hours and relishes the vivid descriptions in fiction books, but I have difficulty staying focused while reading any book that does not have bullet points and pictures. I could go on, but you get the point.

We are unlikely candidates for friendship. Even so, Janna is the sister I spend the most time with and the one involved in my daily life more than any other. If we had merely been two women who met somewhere, our differences might have kept us from choosing to develop a relationship. However, God put us together as sisters, and she has been a wonderful gift to me.

The Lord brings other Sisters into our lives, as well, and we must always be open to these "unlikely" friendships. Blessings often come in unexpected packages.

Because Janna and I are so opposite, our relationship will not thrive unless we both approach it with genuine love and grace. We have to work sometimes to understand each other and see each other's perspectives. We must learn new ways to show love to each other and to meet each other's needs. We both have to put aside our own wills and strive daily to see God's will for each of us individually and in our relationship.

Above all, we must practice daily forgiveness. Even though we are sisters who love each other, we still sometimes hurt each other profoundly. I can recall many moments throughout the years when one of us has said or done something absolutely awful to the other. I am thankful we never used that as an excuse to sever our relationship or to continue acting unkind.

One of our favorites movies in childhood was *Anne of Green Gables*. My sisters and I watched this delightful story of a red-headed girl and all her mischief enough times we had it memorized. One of our favorite quotes from the story is, "Tomorrow is a new day with no mistakes in it yet."[7] All four of us repeat this mantra to our kids and to each other all the time. Its truth has become part of who we are and how we handle life. Of course, it also echoes the Biblical promise that "the Lord's mercies never come to an end; they are new every morning" (Lamentations 3:22-23 ESV).

Since the Lord's forgiveness is endless, then our forgiveness must also be. It cannot be a one-time event; it must have no limit or expiration. As Sisters in Christ, every day, we must wake up with a perspective of starting fresh, a chance to begin again. We cannot hold grudges or let anger find a foothold in our hearts. Instead, we must see every day as an opportunity for change and growth, and wholly forgive each other, no matter how hard that might be.

Ultimately, we must see sisterhood from God's perspective, not a means to an end but rather a spiritual ministry. Sisterhood cannot be about filling the holes in your life, satisfying all your needs, making you feel better about yourself, or getting something from someone. Sure, those things will happen in any godly relationship, but they cannot be the focus or goal.

We must see sisterhood from God's perspective, not a means to an end but rather a spiritual ministry.

As I look back at my relationships with women over the years, I regret so many missed opportunities to show love and compassion to my Sisters in Christ. I can honestly say that I have always had a desire in my heart to love others, but I just haven't always put my desire into action. I think most Christian women *want* to be a good friend, but obstacles get in our way or steer us off course. For me, I focused so much on what others thought of me and how they were affecting my life that I didn't spend much time thinking about them individually.

Even with all the work God has done in me, I still cannot say I am the best Sister in Christ. Sometimes I think about doing a sweet thing for my friend and then get distracted before I accomplish it. Being bold about sharing my faith in everyday situations is still a struggle. When I am not clinging tightly to the Lord, laziness and selfishness can creep into my heart and impact my relationships.

I fall short of being the perfect Sister, but God has made significant changes in my heart regarding women. Most importantly, I now truly see other women as fellow daughters of God, precious and worthy, and I do my best to help my Sisters feel loved and cherished.

While writing this book, I met a woman I can only describe as "different." She did not seem to follow the standard conventions in speech and actions and initially came across as abrupt and disgruntled. When I was younger, I would have done my best to avoid and ignore this woman as I harbored unkind thoughts about her. Thankfully, God's transformation of my heart has opened my eyes. So, I make a point to smile and speak to her whenever I see her.

During one encounter, she broke down in tears over a

specific incident. I sat beside her to give her comfort, so she knew she was not alone.

In our friendship, instead of thinking about how *she* should change to suit me, I contemplate how *I* need to be different and provide her extra special love and compassion.

Being a Sister is so much more than just enjoying a friendship; it is about answering a calling in your life.

We will all meet women who are "different" or maybe even unlikeable. Ultimately, we cannot change any of these women. We must not focus our thoughts or actions on how they treat us, what they think of us, or what need they fulfill for us. Our focus must be on God and how He wants us to show His love to the other women in our lives.

Being a Sister is so much more than just enjoying a friendship; it is about answering a calling in your life.

You often hear people say, "To make a friend, you have to be a friend," and this wise proverb is undoubtedly true. Sisterhood goes beyond that, though. In fact, sisterhood is about removing the first part of this saying and just living out the second part. You just have to be a friend. You are not being a friend in order to get something in return. Your friendship is not conditional.

When I think of my sisters, I am so thankful they never

abandoned me when I couldn't reciprocate the love and service they poured into me. Their commitment to being a sister has never depended on me at all; it is a reflection of their relationship with Christ. This is what being a Sister in Christ is all about. No distance, no situation, no event can make a Sister stop being a Sister. Friends, even close ones, may come and go, but a Sister is a relationship that lasts a lifetime.

So, what is the key to developing this type of lasting, loving relationship? The answer is simple—Christ!

A Sister relationship can endure disappointment, hardship, rudeness, selfishness, and criticism because it is founded on Christ. An unkind word or competitive attitude doesn't shatter this type of friendship because its identity rests solely on God.

A Sister does not depend on her relationships to fill her, save her, or strengthen her. She depends on Jesus.

The bond of Christ holds Christian friends so tightly to each other that nothing can break that bond.

Where do we get the strength to be the Sisters we are called to be? God gives us an abundant amount of strength, wisdom, and grace so we can share His love in our relationships. God provides for us more than we can imagine. He promises us beyond what we could ever hope for. He equips and empowers us to do things we never thought possible. He fills us with His Spirit so much that He can overflow from us to bless those around us. His love and forgiveness never run out, and He wants us to treat our relationships the same way.

In a world where we often feel there is never enough to go around—never enough time to do all we want, never enough money to fund all our dreams, never enough energy to accomplish all our goals—it is comforting to know God promises we will never run out of the most important things. He gives us abundant love and compassion, so there is no limit to how much we can share or the number of Sisters in Christ we can share it with.

God provides us all an endless number of Sisters, and He meets our personal, unique needs through each one of them. I may seek out one for parenting advice. Another may be my exercise buddy. Someone completely different might be the person I call when I have a funny moment to share. There is no need to shop around for the perfect Sister because there is no such thing. Each one of us brings something distinct and special to our Christian family. That's what is beautiful about God and His abundance.

Instead of searching for a friend to meet all my needs, I cherish each Sister God places in my life and look for ways God can use me to share His love with her.

Luke 6:38 is a scripture that comes to mind when I reminisce about life with my biological sisters and the many other women who have been Sisters to me over the years. "Give generously and generous gifts will be given back to you, shaken down to make room for more. <u>Abundant gifts will pour out upon you with such an overflowing measure that it will run over the top!</u> Your measurement of generosity becomes the measurement of your return" (MSG emphasis added). Some people hear this verse as a warning of impending judgment if you are not generous or giving. But I hear an encouraging reminder that God wants to give to us abundantly, and part of how He does that is through our Sisters in Christ. Yes, it takes some work on our part; it takes thoughtful and purposeful action. But what we must give is small compared to the blessings we receive—overflowing, running over the top!

The last time I read Psalm 34, I read it in a completely different way than I had ever read it before. It tells the beautiful testimony of David's faith, and as he lovingly describes the Lord, he urges the hearer to turn toward Him. As I read the scripture, certain powerful words stood out to me, and I could almost hear the voice of my sisters whispering the encouragement directly to me:

> **Come, let us tell of the Lord's greatness; let us exalt his name together.** I prayed to the Lord, and **He answered me**. **He freed me** from all my fears. Those who look to Him for help will be radiant with joy; no shadow of shame will darken their faces. In my desperation, I prayed, and **the Lord listened**; **He saved me** from all my troubles. For the angel of the Lord is a guard; **He surrounds and defends** all who fear

> Him. **Taste and see that the Lord is good.** (Psalm 34:3-8 emphasis added)

When I think about all the sweet Sisters God has given me, I see each one of them with a beautiful smile, a gentleness in her eyes, and her hand outstretched toward me, offering help and encouraging me always to "Taste and see that the Lord is good" (v. 8). They are not perfect. We do not always agree. They can't solve all my problems and may even fail me at times.

My Sisters are real with me. They share their hopes, dreams, and disappointments with me. They serve me unconditionally and are humble enough to let me serve them too. They make a habit of building me up with words of encouragement and truth from God's Word. My Sisters choose to be gracious, forgiving, and encouraging rather than resentful, competitive, or judgmental. They show me by example that this journey of life is so much better together, gently taking me by the hand as we seek together the One who can meet all our needs.

My prayer for each of you is that you experience the joy of having a Sister in Christ and recognize how powerful your presence, words, and testimony are to the women around you.

Tear down any walls that prevent you from connecting with your Sisters. Stand in the gap for other women, being a guard and champion for them during moments of trial or weakness. Choose to freely give grace and don't take personally the wrongs you suffer.

Stop comparing yourself to others, for God made you and all your Sisters uniquely suited to the purpose He has planned for you. Love other women with your words, and be bold in sharing your faith and your story. Make an effort to spend time with your Sisters in Christ, even those who are completely opposite from you.

Show your Sisters in Christ how truly good the Lord is!

Don't allow Satan to convince you that you are not enough, inconvenient, or unimportant, and actively guard against his attempts to keep you isolated or impede you from asking for help.

Know how genuinely loved you are. May you spend each day abiding in Him, who is the only One who can satisfy your needs, and then make it your mission to show your Sisters in Christ how truly good the Lord is!

What Should We Talk About Next?

This book is not an exhaustive look at Christian friendships. It is more of an ice breaker, a conversation starter. *Sister Talk* is not just a catchy phrase; it's a lifestyle. It's about engaging, listening, noticing, and then speaking life into your Christian friendships. It's a decision to live with hopeful enthusiasm for the abundance that can be found in your Sisters in Christ. So what is the next topic of conversation? The answer is up to you...

1. As you've read this book, how has God spoken to your heart about being a Sister in Christ?

2. Is there a particular woman God is calling you to embrace as a Sister?

3. Are there any Sisters you need to forgive or ask for forgiveness from? Ask God to open your eyes to any actions you need to take in this area.

> *This is real love—not that we loved God, but that He loved us and sent His Son as a sacrifice to take away our sins. Dear friends, since God loved us that much, we surely ought to love each other. No one has ever seen God. But if we love each other, God lives in us, and His love is brought to full expression in us.*
>
> *1 John 4: 9-12*

Continue the Conversation

and

Connect with Other Women

Blog: growingbysurprise.com
Facebook: Growing by Surprise

DOWNLOAD A FREE STUDY GUIDE

AND JOURNAL AT:

https://growingbysurprise.com/sister-talk

Acknowledgments

I am incredibly thankful for my three amazing sisters, Janna Binford, Stephanie Jones, and Denise Pitts. Not only did you inspire this book, but you spent hours reviewing, editing, brainstorming, and dreaming with me about it. You kept me focused, always turning my face back to my original vision for this book, and you were my constant cheerleaders. I would never have finished without your support.

To my parents, Neil and Jane Binford, I cannot express enough gratitude for the love, encouragement, and support you have shown me throughout my whole life. You have always inspired me to seek God and follow His will. Because of this, I finally took a leap of faith, followed the Holy Spirit's prompting, and began the journey of writing this book.

My darling husband, Casey, you gave me the space and freedom in our home to pursue my dream and never complained once about fast food dinners, piled laundry, or my incessant talking about this book. Thank you for your help, patience, and faithful support.

Jennifer Breeze, though I have never met you, I feel like you are a close friend. Through your Facebook page, *Christian Author Coaching*, you gave me so much encouragement, advice, direction, and inspiration. Throughout the writing of this book, your posts and comments kept me motivated and gave me great insight into the world of writing.

To another Facebook friend and fellow author, Jennifer Elwood, thanks for all your suggestions, resources, and guidance. When I was at a roadblock, you stepped in and helped me move forward. Your mentorship has been invaluable.

Amber Tinsley, thank you for all your editing help and working diligently under such a time crunch. Your thoughtful comments and critiques were exactly what I needed. Without your help, I never would have finished this book.

To Susan Sage, Karen Weber, Jackie Scott, Aisha Brown, Angie Maes, Sharon Williams, and Jessica Bolyard, I appreciate all the time and effort you took in beta reading this book. You all provided encouragement, insights, and suggestions that helped both motivate and challenge me in my writing.

Flourish Writing Community, you walked me through this process with podcasts, posts, resources, creative ideas, and valuable wisdom, making this writing journey much easier and more enjoyable.

And to anyone who gave me an encouraging word regarding this book, thank you! I am so grateful for all the people God used to motivate and inspire me during this exciting and humbling experience.

About the Author

JENNIFER DUGGER is passionate about helping women see how God can equip and empower them for His mission. As God has called her to unexpected adventures that stretch her beyond her own abilities, she has learned to trust the Lord in all areas of life.

After graduating from Texas A&M University with a math degree, she spent several years teaching high school level math. She also earned her Master of Education in Curriculum and Instruction through Tarleton State University, fully intending to pursue a career as a curriculum director for a local school district. However, through the various twists and turns in life, she adopted three children and now homeschools two of them who have various disabilities.

Inspired to share how God has helped her mature and learn through life's surprising events, she started a blog and Facebook page, *Growing By Surprise*. It is dedicated to encouraging women in their faith and offering hope in the journey for those who have special needs children.

In addition to writing, Jennifer helps coordinate a local American Heritage Girls troop, tutors students in math, and assists with a homeschool co-op. She lives in Texas with her husband and three kids and is blessed with a very loving extended family who lives nearby and supports and encourages her.

Notes

[1] Battistelli, Francesca. *If We're Honest.* 22 Apr. 2014, https://audio-ssl.itunes.apple.com/itunes-assets/AudioPreview62/v4/de/70/a8/de70a854-1680-5f7f-6fa2-e9131e4c632a/mzaf_8683397484006980984.plus.aac.p.m4a.

[2] Mason, Babbie. *Standing In the Gap.* 1 Jan. 1991, https://audio-ssl.itunes.apple.com/itunes-assets/AudioPreview71/v4/71/ae/0e/71ae0ef9-2389-e756-cebc-c2696cb73ac9/mzaf_1561427151387886257.plus.aac.p.m4a.

[3] Gambill, Charlotte. "Walls of Jericho." *Youtube*, Life Church, July 19, 2016. https://youtu.be/LTsTpXUTRUA

[4] Withers, Bill. *Lean On Me.* 1 Jan. 1972, https://audio-ssl.itunes.apple.com/itunes-assets/AudioPreview123/v4/3b/87/f7/3b87f760-3c28-fe9f-1bea-7f5a5cbe123c/mzaf_5391851475138728815.plus.aac.p.m4a.

[5] Mars, Bruno. *Count On Me.* 5 Oct. 2010, https://audio-ssl.itunes.apple.com/itunes-assets/Music/v4/57/37/6e/57376e95-3c47-3773-1451-3dd7ea928094/mzaf_4980861598911230452.plus.aac.p.m4a.

[6] Baum, L. Frank. *The Wonderful Wizard of Oz.* Hesperus Press, 2013.

[7] Montgomery, Lucy Maud. *Anne of Green Gables.* 1908.

Made in the USA
Coppell, TX
17 July 2022